Contents

Chapter 1: Violence Against Women Around the World

Chapter 2: Societal Causes and Effects of Violence Against Women

8 3306611

GLOBALVIEWPOINTS

Violence Against Women

Other Books of Related Interest

PIERCE COLLEGE LIBRARY
PUYALLUP WA 98374
LAKEWOOD WA 98498

GLOBALVIEWPOINTS

Violence Against Women

Kathryn Roberts, Book Editor

GREENHAVEN
PUBLISHING

Published in 2019 by Greenhaven Publishing, LLC
353 3rd Avenue, Suite 255, New York, NY 10010

Copyright © 2019 by Greenhaven Publishing, LLC

First Edition

All rights reserved. No part of this book may be reproduced in any form
without permission in writing from the publisher, except by a reviewer.

Articles in Greenhaven Publishing anthologies are often edited for length to meet page
requirements. In addition, original titles of these works are changed to clearly present
the main thesis and to explicitly indicate the author's opinion. Every effort is made to
ensure that Greenhaven Publishing accurately reflects the original intent of the authors.
Every effort has been made to trace the owners of the copyrighted material.

Cover image: Stefano Montesi/Corbis via Getty Images
Map: frees/Shutterstock.com

Library of Congress Cataloging-in-Publication Data

Names: Roberts, Kathryn, 1990- editor.
Title: Violence against women / Kathryn Roberts, book editor.
Description: New York : Greenhaven Publishing, [2019] | Series: Global
  viewpoints | Audience: Grade 9 to 12. | Includes bibliographical
  references and index.
Identifiers: LCCN 2018028230| ISBN 9781534503922 (library bound) | ISBN
  9781534504714 (pbk.)
Subjects: LCSH: Women—Violence against—Juvenile literature. | Women—Crimes
  against—Juvenile literature. | Women—Crimes
  against—Prevention—Juvenile literature.
Classification: LCC HV6250.4.W65 V521536 2019 | DDC 362.88082—dc23
LC record available at https://lccn.loc.gov/2018028230

Manufactured in the United States of America

Website: http://greenhavenpublishing.com

Not only do El Salvadorian women suffer violence primarily in the home, women and young girls suffer from gang rapes and violent murder under claims that these women and girls are "novias de las pandillas."

Chapter 3: Religion and Violence Against Women

Chapter 4: How to Stop Violence Against Women Around the World

Foreword

"The problems of all of humanity can only be solved by all of humanity."
—*Swiss author Friedrich Dürrenmatt*

G lobal interdependence has become an undeniable reality. Mass media and technology have increased worldwide access to information and created a society of global citizens. Understanding and navigating this global community is a challenge, requiring a high degree of information literacy and a new level of learning sophistication.

Building on the success of its flagship series, Opposing Viewpoints, Greenhaven Publishing has created the Global Viewpoints series to examine a broad range of current, often controversial topics of worldwide importance from a variety of international perspectives. Providing students and other readers with the information they need to explore global connections and think critically about worldwide implications, each Global Viewpoints volume offers a panoramic view of a topic of widespread significance.

Drugs, famine, immigration—a broad, international treatment is essential to do justice to social, environmental, health, and political issues such as these. Junior high, high school, and early college students, as well as general readers, can all use Global Viewpoints anthologies to discern the complexities relating to each issue. Readers will be able to examine unique national perspectives while, at the same time, appreciating the interconnectedness that global priorities bring to all nations and cultures.

Material in each volume is selected from a diverse range of sources, including journals, magazines, newspapers, nonfiction books, speeches, government documents, pamphlets, organization newsletters, and position papers. Global Viewpoints is truly global, with material drawn primarily from international sources available in English and secondarily from U.S. sources with extensive international coverage.

Features of each volume in the Global Viewpoints series include:

- An **annotated table of contents** that provides a brief summary of each essay in the volume, including the name of the country or area covered in the essay.

- An **introduction** specific to the volume topic.

- A **world map** to help readers locate the countries or areas covered in the essays.

- For each viewpoint, an **introduction** that contains notes about the author and source of the viewpoint explains why material from the specific country is being presented, summarizes the main points of the viewpoint, and offers three **guided reading questions** to aid in understanding and comprehension.

- **For further discussion questions** that promote critical thinking by asking the reader to compare and contrast aspects of the viewpoints or draw conclusions about perspectives and arguments.

- A worldwide list of **organizations to contact** for readers seeking additional information.

- A **periodical bibliography** for each chapter and a **bibliography of books** on the volume topic to aid in further research.

- A comprehensive **subject index** to offer access to people, places, events, and subjects cited in the text.

Global Viewpoints is designed for a broad spectrum of readers who want to learn more about current events, history, political science, government, international relations, economics, environmental science, world cultures, and sociology—students doing research for class assignments or debates, teachers and faculty seeking to supplement course materials, and others wanting to understand current issues better. By presenting how people in various countries perceive the root causes, current consequences, and proposed solutions to worldwide challenges, Global Viewpoints volumes offer readers opportunities to enhance their global awareness and their knowledge of cultures worldwide.

Introduction

> *"Violence against women and girls has many faces. One does not have to look far to see these faces, they are all around us. It takes the will to see. It takes the courage to speak up against. It takes the strength to fight against. But inaction is not good enough anymore."*
> —Ewelina U. Ochab, *"The Many Faces of Violence Against Women and Girls,"* Forbes, *November 20, 2017.*

Violence against women comes in many forms and occurs all around the globe. The United Nations defines it as "any act of gender-based violence that results in, or is likely to result in, physical, sexual or mental harm or suffering to women, including threats of such acts, coercion or arbitrary deprivation of liberty, whether occurring in public or in private life." Violence against women—also referred to throughout this text as femicide—is commonly found through domestic violence; emotional, verbal, and financial abuse; street harassment; honor killings; human trafficking; rape; sexual coercion; stalking; and more.

In the United States, domestic violence is one of the top causes of death for women, and in 2005, nearly 1,200 women were murdered by an intimate partner. A recent survey of women in the United States found that most women will experience physical abuse in their lifetime, and a quarter of those women will experience physical abuse or sexual assault from an intimate partner, which makes it one of the highest global rates of domestic violence.

One of the other connections to domestic violence, especially in the United States, is the connections to guns. The United States has one of the highest rates of gun violence around the world, and eighteen percent of mass shooters between 2009 and 2013 had pervious domestic violence charges. Many of the recent mass shootings in the United States, especially those that have taken place at elementary and high schools, have some sort of domestic violence connection.

There are also many societal influences in regard to violence against women. In many countries in Latin and South America, perpetuation of the idea that women belong in the home, taking care of the family, leads to the misconception that a woman is "asking for it" or that she "deserves it" if she is attacked while trying to pursue a career other than homemaker. In countries with histories of military upheaval such as Guatemala, women continue to face violence both inside and outside of the home, with rampant organized crime and gang violence, along with harassment inside the home as women attempt to protect their children from being connected to these gangs.

With the legal marrying age being as young as 15 years old, countries like India grapple not just with women being harassed while taking public transportation, but also with domestic violence related to older men marrying women who are barely more than children. These young women are not capable of supporting themselves and have no choice but to depend on the husbands chosen for them. This has led to a drastic situation of domestic violence situations being underreported in countries like India and Singapore.

Asian countries also must grapple with the "missing women" phenomenon, in which gender discrimination begins at or even before birth. Historically, many families chose to raise only the sons that are born, eventually resulting in a significant shortage of women of childbearing age in countries like China. Without an equal number of women to men, birthrates are likely to drop drastically, which will potentially cause economic upheaval for future generations in that country.

In the Middle East, women and girls suffer from violence simply for stepping out of the home, whether they are pursuing an education or advocating for women's rights. These women face the risk of honor killings and acid attacks, perpetuated by men under the banner of a perverted interpretation of Islam.

Around the world, violence against women comes in many forms, be it acid attacks, dowry-related death, honor killings, street harassment or intimate partner violence. There is much debate as to the best ways to curb it. Religious-based attacks on women are prevalent all over the world, as are attacks on women used as a tool of ongoing war in many developing countries. Shedding light on this situation that impacts nearly every single girl and woman on the planet, the contributors in *Global Viewpoints: Violence Against Women* explore the causes of and solutions to violence against women.

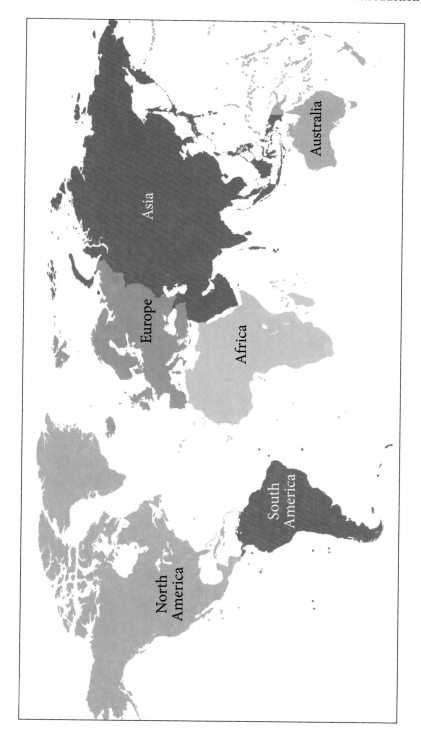

GLOBAL VIEWPOINTS

CHAPTER 1

Violence Against Women Around the World

1960s Feminism Shines a Light on Violence Against Women

Tavaana

In the following viewpoint, writers from Tavaana detail the history of the feminist movement of the 1960s and 1970s, including women-led attempts to curb gender discrimination and allow women to have more rights both inside and outside of the home. Prior to the earnest beginnings of this movement, women followed a fairly traditional path of graduating from college, marrying early, and working more-than-full-time hours caring for the home and children. These women were unable to control their own finances, were forced to submit to the will of their husbands, and found it extremely difficult to end unsuccessful or abusive marriages. Tavaana supports active citizenship and civic leadership in Iran through a multi-platform civic education and civil society capacity building program.

As you read, consider the following questions:

1. What made it difficult for women to receive a divorce in the 1960s?
2. What did women do in their attempts for equality? Which actions were the most successful?
3. When was sexual harassment legally defined as a violation of women's rights?

"The 1960s-70s American Feminist Movement: Breaking Down Barriers for Women," Tavaana, E-Collaborative for Civic Education. Reprinted by permission.

In 1960, the world of American women was limited in almost every respect, from family life to the workplace. A woman was expected to follow one path: to marry in her early 20s, start a family quickly, and devote her life to homemaking. As one woman at the time put it, "The female doesn't really expect a lot from life. She's here as someone's keeper—her husband's or her children's."[1] As such, wives bore the full load of housekeeping and child care, spending an average of 55 hours a week on domestic chores.[2] They were legally subject to their husbands via "head and master laws," and they had no legal right to any of their husbands' earnings or property, aside from a limited right to "proper support"; husbands, however, would control their wives' property and earnings.[3] If the marriage deteriorated, divorce was difficult to obtain, as "no-fault" divorce was not an option, forcing women to prove wrongdoing on the part of their husbands in order to get divorced.[4]

The 38 percent of American women who worked in 1960 were largely limited to jobs as teacher, nurse, or secretary.[5] Women were generally unwelcome in professional programs; as one medical school dean declared, "Hell yes, we have a quota...We do keep women out, when we can. We don't want them here—and they don't want them elsewhere, either, whether or not they'll admit it."[6] As a result, in 1960, women accounted for six percent of American doctors, three percent of lawyers, and less than one percent of engineers.[7] Working women were routinely paid lower salaries than men and denied opportunities to advance, as employers assumed they would soon become pregnant and quit their jobs, and that, unlike men, they did not have families to support.

In 1962, Betty Friedan's book *The Feminine Mystique* captured the frustration and even the despair of a generation of college-educated housewives who felt trapped and unfulfilled. As one said, "I'm desperate. I begin to feel I have no personality. I'm a server of food and a putter-on of pants and a bedmaker, somebody who can be called on when you want something. But who am I?"[8] Friedan stunned the nation by contradicting the accepted wisdom that housewives were content to serve their families and by calling on women to seek fulfillment in work outside the home. While Friedan's writing largely spoke to an audience of educated, upper-middle-class white women, her work had such an impact that it is credited with sparking the "second wave" of the American feminist movement. Decades earlier, the "first wave" had pushed for women's suffrage, culminating with the passage of the 19th Amendment that gave women the right to vote in 1920. Now a new generation would take up the call for equality beyond the law and into women's lives.

Goals and Objectives

The feminist movement of the 1960s and '70s originally focused on dismantling workplace inequality, such as denial of access to better jobs and salary inequity, via anti-discrimination laws. In 1964, Representative Howard Smith of Virginia proposed to add a prohibition on gender discrimination into the Civil Rights Act that was under consideration. He was greeted by laughter from the other Congressmen, but with leadership from Representative Martha Griffiths of Michigan, the law passed with the amendment intact.[9]

However, it quickly became clear that the newly established Equal Employment Opportunity Commission would not enforce the law's protection of women workers, and so a group of feminists including Betty Friedan decided to found an organization that would fight gender discrimination through the courts and legislatures. In the summer of 1966, they launched the National Organization for Women (NOW), which went on to lobby Congress for pro-equality laws and assist women seeking legal aid as they battled workplace discrimination in the courts.[10]

As such, Betty Friedan's generation sought not to dismantle the prevailing system but to open it up for women's participation on a public, political level. However, the more radical "women's liberation" movement was determined to completely overthrow the patriarchy that they believed was oppressing every facet of women's lives, including their private lives.[11] They popularized the idea that "the personal is political"—that women's political inequality had equally important personal ramifications, encompassing their relationships, sexuality, birth control and abortion, clothing and body image, and roles in marriage, housework and childcare.[12] As such, the different wings of the feminist movement sought women's equality on both a political and personal level.

Leadership

The feminist movement was not rigidly structured or led by a single figure or group. As one feminist wrote, "The women's movement is a non-hierarchical one. It does things collectively and experimentally."[13] In fact, the movement was deeply divided between young and old, upper-class and lower-class, conservative and radical. Betty Friedan was determined to make the movement a respectable part of mainstream society and distanced herself from what she termed the "bra-burning, anti-man, politics-of-orgasm" school of feminism; she even spent years insinuating that the young feminist leader Gloria Steinem had sinister links to the FBI and CIA.[14] Younger feminists, for their part, distrusted the older generation and viewed NOW as stuffy and out of touch: "NOW's demands and organizational style weren't radical enough for us."[15]

When these divides were combined with a reluctance to choose official leaders for the movement, it gave the media an opening to anoint its own "feminist leaders," leading to resentment within the movement. Meanwhile, in this leadership vacuum, the most assertive women promoted themselves as leaders, prompting attacks from other women who believed that all members of the movement should be equal in status.[16]

Nonetheless, women like Gloria Steinem and Germaine Greer attracted media attention through both their popular writings and their appealing image. They played a key role representing feminism to the public and the media—providing attractive examples of women who were feminists without fitting the negative stereotypes of humorless, ugly, man-hating shrews.[17]

Civic Environment

In large part, the success of the feminist movement was driven by a favorable confluence of economic and societal changes. After World War II, the boom of the American economy outpaced the available workforce, making it necessary for women to fill new job openings; in fact, in the 1960s, two-thirds of all new jobs went to women.[18] As such, the nation simply had to accept the idea of women in the workforce. Meanwhile, as expectations for a comfortable middle-class lifestyle rose, having two incomes became critical to achieving this lifestyle, making women's participation in the workforce still more acceptable.[19]

But many of these women were relegated to low-paying clerical and administrative work. What opened the door for women to pursue professional careers was access to the Pill—reliable oral contraception. Knowing that they could now complete years of training or study and launch their career without being interrupted by pregnancy, a wave of young women began applying to medical, law, and business schools in the early 1970s. At the same time, the Pill made the "sexual revolution" possible, helping to break down the double standard that allowed premarital sex for men but prohibited it for women.

Feminist leaders were also inspired by the Civil Rights movement, through which many of them had gained civic organizing experience. At the same time, black women played a key role in the Civil Rights movement, especially through local organizations, but were shut out of leadership roles.[20] Meanwhile, the women's anti-war movement was joined by a new generation of more radical young women protesting not only the Vietnam war but also "the way in which the traditional women's peace movement condoned and even enforced the gender hierarchy in which men made war and women wept."[21] On college campuses, women joined in the leftist student movement, but their efforts to incorporate women's rights into the New Left were ignored or met with condescension from the male student leaders; at one New Politics conference, the chairman told a feminist activist, "Cool down, little girl. We have more important things to do here than talk about women's problems."[22] As a result, women split off from the movements that marginalized them in order to form their own movement.

At the same time, the FBI viewed the women's movement as "part of the enemy, a challenge to American values," as well as potentially violent and linked to other "extremist" movements.[23] It paid hundreds of female informants across the country to infiltrate the women's movement.[24] While this infiltration intensified paranoia and eroded trust among activists, it did not change the course of the movement as it continued to fight for equal rights.[25]

Message and Audience

The women's movement used different means to strive for equality: lobbying Congress to change laws; publicizing issues like rape and domestic violence through the media; and reaching out to ordinary women to both expand the movement and raise their awareness of how feminism could help them.

Early in the women's liberation movement, which was deeply rooted in the New Left, activists took an aggressive approach to their protests. Protests against sexism in the media ranged from putting stickers saying "Sexist" on offensive advertisements to holding sit-ins at local media outlets, all the way to sabotage of newspaper offices.[26] This approach sometimes crossed the line into offensiveness, as at the 1968 demonstration outside the Miss America pageant in Atlantic City, where activists protested objectification of women by waving derogatory signs like "Up Against the Wall, Miss America." While the event attracted widespread media coverage (and launched the myth that feminists burned bras), the approach was alienating. As a result, many activists resolved to "stop using the 'in-talk' of the New Left/ Hippie movement" and strive to reach ordinary women across the country.[27]

"Consciousness-raising groups" became an effective way to do so; in small groups in local communities, women explored topics such as family life, education, sex, and work from their personal perspectives. As they shared their stories, they began to understand themselves in relation to the patriarchal society they lived in, and they discovered their commonalities and built solidarity; as one said, "[I began to] see myself as part of a larger population of women. My circumstances are not unique, but...can be traced to the social structure."[28]

Meanwhile, in their campaigns for the legalization of abortion, activists testified before state legislatures and held public "speak-outs" where women admitted to illegal abortions and explained their reasons for abortion; these events "brought abortion out of the closet where it had been hidden in secrecy and shame. It informed the public that most women were having abortions anyway. People spoke from their hearts. It was heart-rending."[29] The "speak-out" was also used to publicize the largely unacknowledged phenomenon of rape, as activists also set up rape crisis centers and advocacy groups, and lobbied police departments and hospitals to treat rape victims with more sensitivity.[30] To publicize date rape, the annual "Take Back the Night" march on college campuses was launched in 1982.[31]

Activists also defined and campaigned against sexual harassment, which was legally defined as a violation of women's rights in 1980; they also redefined spousal abuse as not a tradition but a crime, lobbied for legal change, and set up domestic violence shelters.[32] The women's health movement set up a new goal of creating a women-centered health system, rather than the existing system that was often insensitive to women's needs; activists educated themselves on the female body, began giving classes in homes, daycares, and churches, set up women's clinics, and published the reference book *Our Bodies, Ourselves*.[33]

Meanwhile, the women's movement was producing a huge number of journals in local communities across the country. While these journals were produced largely for members of the movement, Gloria Steinem's *Ms.* Magazine, founded in 1971, expanded the audience to the general public at a national level. It publicized the problems ordinary women faced, published inspirational stories of successful women, and covered grassroots activist efforts across the country.[34]

At the same time, the movement used class action lawsuits, formal complaints, protests, and hearings to create legal change.[35] By the late 1970s, they had made tangible, far reaching gains, including the outlawing of gender discrimination in education, college sports, and obtaining financial credit[36]; the banning of employment discrimination against pregnant women[37]; the legalization of abortion[38] and birth control[39]; and the establishment of "irreconcilable differences" as grounds for divorce and equalization of property division during divorce.[40] Members of the women's movement were invigorated by these successes; as one said, "I knew I was a part of making history...It gave you a real high, because you knew real things could come out of it."[41]

The August 1970 Women's Strike for Equality, a nationwide wave of protests, marches, and sit-ins, captured this spirit of optimism. However, it soon gave way to a backlash exemplified by the failure of the Equal Rights Amendment (ERA), a proposed constitutional amendment that would protect women's rights. It swiftly passed Congress in 1972 and was ratified by 30 states by the end of the following year. Still, it was unable to gain the 8 additional ratifications necessary by the 1982 deadline. At first there was widespread public support for the ERA by a margin of at least two to one—in theory, at least.[42] In practice, the public was still very conservative when it came to men's and women's roles, and a growing backlash against the changes feminism represented coincided with a backlash against gay rights and abortion rights, as led by the newly ascendant conservative movement, particularly the Christian right wing.

Moreover, the women's movement failed to communicate the benefits of the ERA; by the time it passed Congress, many of the inequalities in the country's laws had already been addressed, and it was hard for the public to see what positive impact the amendment could have.[43] The ERA's opponents, on the other hand, painted a vivid picture of the terrible effects the ERA could have on the country. They attacked it as a plot to dismantle the foundations of American society, especially the family, and denounced the ERA's "hidden agenda": "taxpayer funding of abortions and the entire gay rights agenda."[44] The ERA's leading opponent, Phyllis Schlafly, denied that women were discriminated against at all; rather, she said, they enjoyed a sanctified position in American society through the "Christian tradition of chivalry," which the ERA would destroy.[45] While the ERA failed, and the backlash against feminism has continued, the struggle for women's rights has also continued, leaving a lasting impact on American society.

Outreach Activities

Due to the cross-cutting nature of the women's movement, which included women who were already members of other movements, it was naturally suited to build links with these movements. For instance, some members of the feminist movement traveled abroad to meet Vietnamese women who were against the war in that country, in an effort to build sisterly anti-war solidarity.[46] Meanwhile, feminists with roots in the labor movement launched local groups to organize women workers, improve their working conditions, and fight for their equal rights on the job.[47] Black feminists targeted such issues as child care, police repression, welfare, and healthcare, and founded the National Black Feminist Organization in 1973.[48]

By the end of the 1970s, activists burned out, and the women's movement fragmented—but the services they founded, such as rape crisis centers, women's shelters, and health clinics, were integrated into the mainstream as cities, universities, and religious organizations provided program funding.[49] Today the gains of the feminist movement—women's equal access to education, their increased participation in politics and the workplace, their access to abortion and birth control, the existence of resources to aid domestic violence and rape victims, and the legal protection of women's rights—are often taken for granted. While feminists continue to strive for increased equality, as Betty Friedan wrote, "What used to be the feminist agenda is now an everyday reality. The way women look at themselves, the way other people look at women, is completely different...than it was thirty years ago ... Our daughters grow up with the same possibilities as our sons."[50]

Notes

1. Coontz, Stephanie. *A Strange Stirring: The Feminine Mystique and American Women at the Dawn of the 1960s.* New York: Basic Books, 2011. 42.
2. Coontz, Stephanie. "When We Hated Mom." *New York Times.* 7 May. 2011.
3. *A Strange Stirring* 46.
4. Collins, Gail. *When Everything Changed: The Amazing Journey of American Women from 1960 to the Present.* New York: Little, Brown & Company, 2009. 43.
5. "100 Years of Consumer Spending: 1960-61." Bureau of Labor Statistics. 2006. PDF.
6. Collins 38.
7. Ibid.
8. Collins 117.
9. Ibid. 149-160.
10. Ibid. 165-168.
11. Ibid. 368-9.
12. Rosen, Ruth. *The World Split Open: How the Modern Women's Movement Changed America.* New York: Viking Penguin, 2000. 196.
13. Collins 388.
14. Sullivan, Patricia. "Voice of Feminism's 'Second Wave.'" *Washington Post.* 5 Feb. 2006.
15. Rosen 84, 88.
16. Ibid. 227-9.
17. Ibid. 154, 217.
18. Collins 194.
19. Ibid. 199.
20. Ibid. 238.
21. Ibid. 367.
22. Ibid. 372-3.
23. Rosen 245-6.
24. Ibid. 241.
25. Ibid. 259-60.
26. Ibid. 162.
27. Ibid. 161.
28. Ibid. 197, 248.
29. Ibid. 158.
30. Ibid. 182.
31. Ibid. 184.
32. Ibid. 186-7.

33. Ibid. 176.

34. Ibid. 211, 216.

35. Ibid. 88-90.

36. Title IX of the Education Amendments (1972); the Equal Credit Opportunity Act (1974).

37. The Pregnancy Discrimination Act (1978).

38. The *Roe v. Wade* Supreme Court decision (1973).

39. The *Eisenstadt v. Baird* Supreme Court ruling (1972).

40. The Uniform Marriage and Divorce Act (1970), passed by the US Uniform Law Commission, which strongly influenced state laws.

41. Rosen 200.

42. Daniels, Mark R., Robert Darcy, and Joseph W. Westphal. "The ERA Won—At Least in the Opinion Polls." *PS: Political Science and Politics* 15:4 (Autumn 1982), American Political Science Association.

43. Collins 444.

44. Schlafly, Phyllis. "'Equal Rights' For Women: Wrong Then, Wrong Now." *Los Angeles Times*, 8 April 2007.

45. Collins 451.

46. Rosen 137-8.

47. Ibid. 268-9.

48. Ibid. 282-4.

49. Ibid. 270.

50. Friedan, Betty. *Life So Far: A Memoir.* New York: Touchstone, 2000. 375.

In Latin America Femicide Rates Are Higher

Celeste Saccomano

In the following viewpoint, an excerpt from a larger piece concerning femicide in Latin American countries, Celeste Saccomano details the global rates of violence against women, specifically in Western Europe and Latin America, where the rates are significantly higher. After defining femicide, along with discussing the murder of young girls and children, the author details the causes and socioecological theories behind these types of violence. Additionally she concludes with thoughts on the lack of action taken politically and how that will continue to impact the rates of violence in these countries. Saccomano is a policy and legal analyst specializing in gender-based violence.

As you read, consider the following questions:

1. When did Latin American countries begin attempting to combat the high rates of violence and discrimination against women?
2. What caused the rates of femicide to fluctuate in Latin American countries, even as its governments took measures to curb the violence?
3. Why are the rates of intimate partner homicide so high in Latin American countries?

"The Causes of Femicide in Latin America," by Celeste Saccomano, Institut Barcelona d'Estudis Internacionals (IBEI). Reprinted by permission.

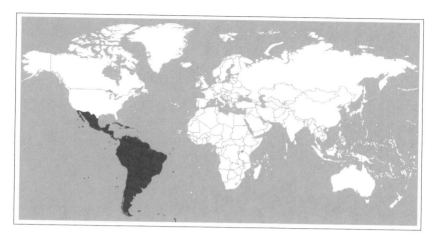

Violence against women (thereinafter VAW) has been recognized as an increasing problem in today's society: it is a violation of human rights, a social problem, a public health problem and a barrier to economic development for countries (Bott, Guedes, Goodwin & Mendoza, 2013, p.5). Femicide is the most extreme expression of VAW, the "killing of women by men motivated by hate, contempt, pleasure or the assumption of ownership of women" (Russell, 2008, p.2), and encompasses any women homicides committed on the basis of gender discrimination. According to the World Health Organization report "Global and Regional Estimates of VAW," if the Western Europe region has a prevalence of intimate partner violence of 19.3%, the Latin America region has sensibly higher rates: 40.63% in the Andean area, 29.51% in Central Latin America, and 23.68% in Southern Latin America ([WHO], 2013, p. 47).

Because of the high femicide rates and as a response to internal and external pressure, Latin American countries started to take action against violence and discrimination against women in the second half of the 1990s. These actions followed one of the two most important international conventions[1] for protection of women's rights, the Convention of Belém do Pará. Since then, Latin American countries went through a process of increasing legislation and regulation of crimes against women. The process entailed two generations of legislation which provided a more comprehensive, multidimensional, and multi sectoral approach to fighting gender-based crime through increase and expansion of regulation (Garita, 2011, p. 11). The second generation started around 2007, and mainly consisted of the implementation of laws which typify gender-based homicide as a separate and more serious criminal offense called specifically "femicide." The international community, as well as Women and Human Rights movements have celebrated the reach of such milestone, because they expected that the number of femicides would drop as a consequence of the legislation.

However, while in some cases the femicide rate decreased, in others it increased and in yet others it initially decreased only to increase again. Indeed, there is also high variation in the number of femicides among countries that have typified the criminal offense and have engaged in campaigns to raise popular awareness against gender-based violence.

Thus, this paper tries to understand why femicide rates have not responded homogeneously to the adoption of such laws, and more specifically, it aims at finding the factors that are related to the rise and fall of femicide numbers. Thus, I will analyze the variation in the rate of femicides in 14 countries in Latin America.

In a nutshell, by looking at the rates of femicides in 14 Latin American countries over the period 2000-2014, I find that the level of rule of law as well as the proportion of seats held by women in national parliaments and female percentage of total labour force in a country matter for predicting the number of femicides in a country. Furthermore, I find that the typification of the crime, minimum and maximum mandatory sentencing, level of female education and public expenditures on education and health do not matter when analyzing rates of femicide.

This study fills a gap in the literature by bringing together feminists and sociological theories and applying them to the Latin American reality. It also evaluates, through a comparative regional perspective, the situation of extreme violence against women

El Salvador's Shameful Record with Women

Visiting United Nations human rights chief has urged El Salvador to address issues faced by women such as having the femicide and an abortion ban that punishes women "for apparent miscarriages and obstetric emergencies."

"El Salvador has the awful distinction of having the highest rate of gender-based killings of women and girls in Central America—a region where femicide is already regrettably high, as is impunity for these crimes," said UN High Commissioner for Human Rights Zeid Ra'ad Al Hussein in his end-of-mission statement.

The country has reported 575 brutal killings of women in 2015, with almost 45 percent of the murdered women being under the age of 30. Only a fourth of such cases are prosecuted in the country where gang violence is so rampant.

Between January 2015 to February 2017 the country has seen deaths of a thousand civilians and 45 police officers in armed confrontations between the police and alleged gang members.

The country has an absolute ban on abortion. It has often led to situations such as women being convicted of "aggravated homicide" in connection with obstetric emergencies serving 30 years in prison.

Hussein called for a moratorium on the abortion ban and review of all detentions under abortion-related offences.

"El-Salvador Urged to Address High Rate of Femicide, Abortion Ban," Development Channel, November 18, 2017.

and the existing advances on femicides in the evolving fields of legislation and human development in the region.

[…]

What Is Femicide?

One of the most important tasks when talking about femicide is to clarify its difference from woman homicide. While Female Homicide is any murder of women or girls regardless of the circumstances, Femicide is the murder of women or girls for gender-based reasons (Bloom, 2008, p.176). A Female Homicide can be classified as Femicide by investigating the circumstances of death and the relationship existing between the victim and the murderer (Bloom, 2008, p.176). Among the different types of femicide, the murder of an intimate partner (Intimate Partner Femicide) and the murder of a woman preceded by sexual violation (Non-Intimate Sexual Femicide) are the most common in Latin America (Toledo, 2008, p.213; WHO, 2012, p.3).

The concept of femicide goes back to 1900. In fact, according to femicide specialist Diana Russell, the term femicide was first used in the UK in 1801 to signify "the killing of a woman" (2008, p.3). However, the neologism remained unused until the 1970s, when it gained relevance thanks to the feminist movements, which reintroduced it and politicized it in an effort to draw attention to the harmful effects of gender inequality (UN Human Rights Council [UNHRC], 2012b, p.6)

The responsability for the renaissance of the term in the United States is the feminist writer and activist Diana Russell. After using it for the first time in a written declaration at the Tribunal on Crimes Against Women in 1976, she defined it, together with Harmes in 1992, as "the misogynous killing of women by men" and in 2001 as "the killing of females by males because they are female," substituting "female" for "women" in order to encompass all girls and female babies killed (Russell, 2008, p.2).

Femicide in Latin America: Femicidio and Feminicidio

The arrival of the concept in Latin America was welcomed by their fellow feminists. When translating it into Spanish, the vocable underwent an interesting formal and theoretical modification, which aimed at a better understanding of the Latin American reality. The Mexican feminist activist Marcela Lagarde decided to use the neologism feminicidio instead of translating it literally to the Spanish femicidio, to add the element of impunity, institutional violence and lack of due diligence by Latin America toward women. (Lagarde, 2006, p.223)[2].

Title: Figure 1. Violence Against Women and Femicide: A Typology of Violence

Violence

Nature of violence	Self-Directed		Interpersonal					Collective		
	Suicidal behavior	Self-abuse	Family/partner			Community		Social	Political	Economic
			Child	Partner	Elder	Acquaintance	Stranger			
Physical	X	X	X	X	X	X	X	X	X	X
Sexual			X	X	X	X	X	X	X	X
Psychological	X	X	X	X	X	X	X	X	X	X
Deprivation or neglect	X	X	X	X	X	X	X	X	X	X

In order to understand femicide we need to consider the context of VAW. Indeed, femicide is in most cases the "end of a continuum of violence against women, set against general patterns of discrimination against women and tolerated impunity of perpetrators" (UNHRC, 2012a, p. 10).

Figure 1 shows the different types of violence in relation to the perpetrator and to its nature (Krug et al., 2002). First, it encompasses Self-directed violence, usually as a result of gender violence such as suicide-femicide. Second, it includes Collective violence, committed by large groups such as militia and terrorist groups. Third, it comprises Interpersonal violence, which is the more typical type of VAW. The latter is subcategorized into Family, Intimate Partner Violence, and Community Violence. Family and Intimate Partner Violence is inflicted "between family members and intimate partners, usually, though not exclusively, taking place in the home" and femicide has been found to be in most cases its lethal result (Krug et al., 2002, p.6). A global study on intimate partner violence confirmed that women are up to 6 times more affected than men by "intimate partner homicide" (respectively 38,6% vs 6.3%), and that the region of the Americas 38% ranked only second after South East Asia (58,8%) (Stöckl H et al., 2013, p.862). Finally, Community Violence is violence "between individuals who are unrelated, who may or may not know each other and generally takes place outside the home" and includes rape or sexual assault by strangers, and violence in institutional settings (WHO, 2002, p.6).

[…]

What Do We Know About Femicide and Its Causes?

Femicide has been investigated from different perspectives and throughout a variety of disciplines, such as psychology, sociology, and political movements. To understand femicides, we need to understand how each discipline has framed and analyzed the problem.

Latin American Feminists theorizers (Lagarde, 2008; Carcedo, 2000; Toledo, 2009) explained VAW as consequence of gender inequality, society structures such as patriarchy, impunity and institutional violence. Feminists laid down the foundations to sociological-feminist studies which investigated the phenomena of femicide through gender lenses (Monárrez 2009; Vera, 2012; Prieto-Carrón, Thomson & Macdonald, 2007; Ariza Sosa, 2012).

Sociology studies have analyzed femicide trends in relation to a variety of social circumstances (Lagarde, 2008, p.212), but among them, particularly relevant for this investigation have been those which explore VAW as a public health problem (Arias, 2008; Heise, Pitanguy & Germain, 1994) and those which, drawing from all the previous theories, considered both individual and social variables as causal factors of VAW and femicide: Ecological theorists (Heise, 1998; Krug et al.,2002; WHO, 2012; WHO, 2103; UN Women, n.d.). Finally, there are critical studies which focus on the construction of sex disaggregated indicators (Castro & Riquer, 2003), and argue that claims on femicide increasing rates are unfounded given that Latin American countries do not have the capacity of building databases that assess gender motivation (Tuesta & Mujica, 2014, p.2).

[...]

Socio-ecological Theories

Socioecological theories are important because they depart from the understanding that VAW is the result not only of singular individual, sociocultural or situational factors but also the outcome of the multidimensional interplay among all of them. The Ecological Model is the sociological framework used nowadays by international organizations to understand the causes of crime and VAW. It has also been applied to understand Intimate partner violence (Heise, 1998; Krug et al., 2002) and femicide (WHO, 2012).

The ecological framework identifies many causes of VAW. At the individual level, the important factors are: Witnessing martial violence as a child, being abused oneself as a child, having an absent or rejecting father (Heise, 1998), young age, alcohol abuse, personality disorders, low academic achievement, low income, history of violence in family (Krug et al., 2002, p.98). Second, relationships factors involve Male dominance in the family, Male control of wealth in the family, marital verbal conflict (Heise, 1998, p.265), economic stress, and instability (Krug et al., 2002, p.98). Third, community factors involve Low socioeconomic status or unemployment, Isolation of woman and family, Delinquent peer associations (Heise, 1998, p. 265), poverty, and low social capital (Krug et al., 2002, p.98). Fourth, Social factors are Sense of male entitlement/ownership of women, Masculinity linked to dominance, Rigid gender roles, Acceptance of Interpersonal violence and Physical chastisement. (Heise, 1998, p.265) Traditional gender norms and social norms supportive of violence, Weak community sanctions against domestic violence (Krug et al., 2002, p.98).

When the ecological model was applied specifically to Femicide, a few more factors were identified as important: low number of women in elected government, reductions in government social spending on areas such as health and education, Prior intimate partner abuse, no mandated arrest for violation of restraining orders related to intimate partner violence, no legislation restricting access to firearms for perpetrators of intimate partner violence, gun ownership, threats to kill with a weapon, forcing sexual intercourse with a partner, problematic alcohol use and drug use, mental health problems, (WHO, 2012, p.4).

The comprehensive and multidimensional approach taken by the Ecological Method is confirmed by scientific investigations on mortality in the field of public health. Arias (2006, p.125) claimed that violent deaths by homicides are avoidable, as demonstrated by industrialized countries which have sensibly reduced homicides by preventive public policies aimed at reducing social inequalities through control of their social, cultural and economic determinants (p.83).

UN Women (n.d.) draws from all the aforementioned theories and bases its policy making on the causes identified through the

Ecological framework. In addition to all the variables previously cited the organization also identifies as risk factors disparity between men and women in education and employment, lack of safe spaces for women and girls and low level of awareness among health and justice service providers (n.d.). According to its focus on women's empowerment, UN Women emphasizes low women participation in decision making as a risk factor (2013, p.35).

[…]

Conclusion

In this study, I have illustrated the problem of extreme gender violence in Latin America with the aim of individuate the causes behind variation in femicide rates. I started by defining the difference between femicide and women homicide, and explaining the history of the concept. Then, I mentioned the importance that the term acquired in Latin America as a political response to institutional violence and impunity, and how this movement, together with international organizations for human's rights, achieved the implementation into national legislation of laws typifying femicide by a growing number of countries. While reviewing feminists and sociologists literature, I individuated their position on the causes of femicide: while the first one claimed structural gender inequality and impunity the main cause of the perpetuation of extreme gender violence, the latter argued that it is a problem that needs to be addressed at multiple levels. On such basis I formulated three hypotheses aimed at explaining the most important factors influencing femicide trends in Latin American countries: particular features of regulation, impunity and gender inequality. Finally, I illustrated the results obtained through linear regression analysis, that is that the variables that proved significant to variation in femicide rate were levels of Rule of Law, low levels of Control of corruption, and percentage of seats held by women in national parliaments. I conclude by clarifying that prioritizing the fight against impunity as way to end extreme gender violence, however, does not mean that legislation and regulation aimed at the protection and empowerment of women should not be implemented, but simply that in the region of Latin America, until impunity won't be fought, its positive efforts may be neutralized.

Notes

1. Namely, the Convention on the Elimination of All Forms of Discrimination against Women, adopted in 1979 by the UN General Assembly and the Inter-American Convention on the Prevention, Punishment, and Eradication of VAW approved in 1994 by the Organization of American States, also called Convention of Belém do Pará.
2. However, because of the fast spread and popularization of the word thanks to the media and the feminist movement, there is a general confusion and inconsistency in its use, and the word feminicide is often misplaced to indicate any woman killing (Lagarde, 2008, p.218).

In India It's Entirely Legal for a Man to Rape His Wife

Katie Dallas

In the following viewpoint, Katie Dallas of the Global Poverty Project interviews Trisha Shetty of the nonprofit organization SheSays about marital rape around the world and seeking the end of gender-based discrimination in countries like India, a country in which marital rape is legal, even for girls as young as fifteen years old. Throughout the interview, Dallas and Shetty detail the impact anti-violence advocacy has on the advocates, and the harassment these advocates face online and in the media.

As you read, consider the following questions:

1. Why is it legal in so many countries for a man to rape his wife?
2. Per the viewpoint, how many men in India have admitted to having forced sexual acts on their wives?
3. Why is it so difficult to advocate for the end of marital rape laws? Explain your reasoning.

"Interview with Trisha Shetty: 'Why It's Entirely Legal for a Man to Rape His Wife in India,'" by Katie Dallas, Global Poverty Project, Inc., March 7, 2017. Reprinted by permission.

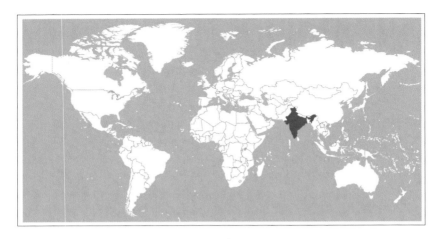

In India's constitution, under The Criminal Law (Amendment) Act of 2013, you can find the chilling statement: "Sexual intercourse or sexual acts by a man with his own wife, the wife not being under fifteen years of age, is not rape."

India is not alone. There are 48 other nations today where a husband can legally rape his wife. In Singapore, for example, a man is not guilty of rape if the victim is his spouse and over the age of 13.

Since marital rape is not a crime in India, precise numbers are hard to come by. However, a survey conducted in 2014 with over 9,000 men across seven Indian states revealed the magnitude of the problem: a staggering one in three of those men admitted to having forced a sexual act on their wives.

In a country where 65% of women agree that "there are times when a woman deserves to be beaten," the path to criminalization of marital rape is an extremely complex one.

In the week leading up to International Women's Day, Global Citizen caught up with Trisha Shetty, one of the key players fighting to change the law in India. Shetty is a lawyer, activist, and founder of SheSays—a nonprofit seeking to end gender-based discrimination and advance women's rights in India. The organization's educational website receives thousands of visits a day from abused women who have nowhere else to go for support.

What has been the hardest obstacle you have had to contend with so far in your advocacy campaign to outlaw marital rape?

There are so many but certainly the toughness of the opposition is up there—the hostile climate around this issue is intense and can be wearing.

I am pretty vocal as a campaigner against all sorts of conservative ideologies that discriminate against women and yet I have never been as harassed online as I have when I talk about this issue. In response to one particular comment I made that "Marriage is not a license for sex," I have faced systematic targeting on all channels across Twitter, Facebook, Youtube—with trolls posting offensive pictures of me, relentlessly stalking me and men threatening to rape me.

To put it in perspective—in 2013, post the brutal gang rape that received worldwide attention, the Criminal Law Amendment Act came through, where they changed the definition of rape and declared various acts such as stalking as a legal offense. Marital rape was also recommended to be a crime by the justice committee that introduced the Act and yet that was the only thing that was taken out. So the lawmakers chose to not recognize that raping your wife is a crime.

How could there be any legal justification to keep marital rape legal?

There are a few common lines of argument they keep throwing out, which all stem from a claim that criminalizing marital rape will lead to a proliferation of fake rape cases.

The first is "Should I sign a consent form every time I have sex with my wife? To say this is consensual so she doesn't file a rape charge at me later?" And the second is "Will you install cameras in the marital bedroom now? How will you prove it?"

Some also cite the low conviction rate for rape cases—which sits at around 29% in India—as evidence of the high number of

Femicide Is a Global Problem

Rates of femicide—acts of homicide in which the victim is a woman or a girl—are significantly higher in countries and territories affected by high or very high overall homicide rates. With a rate of 12.0 per 100,000 people, El Salvador is the country with the highest femicide rate, followed by Jamaica (10.9), Guatemala (9.7), and South Africa (9.6).

Femicide: A Global Problem, the latest Research Note from the Small Arms Survey, offers a concise examination of lethal forms of violence against women, drawing on the disaggregated data on femicides produced for the Global Burden of Armed Violence 2011, published by the Geneva Declaration on Armed Violence and Development.

About 66,000 women and girls are violently killed every year, accounting for approximately 17 per cent of all victims of intentional homicides. In countries marked by high levels of lethal violence, women are more frequently attacked in the public sphere; in this context, femicides often take place in a general climate of indifference and impunity.

The regions with the highest femicide levels largely correspond to the regions with the highest overall rates of lethal violence. Eastern Europe and the Russian Federation, however, show disproportionally high rates of femicide with respect to homicides in general.

Firearms play an important role in lethal violence, and the display of firearms—as a means to intimidate, threaten, or coerce someone—is a predictor of their actual use.

Intimate partner violence is widespread and, as part of an abusive relationship, it can easily become lethal. Prolonged exposure to intolerable levels of violence at home can also lead a victim to commit 'forced suicide'.

Accurate information is a key to understanding the characteristics of femicide and to developing sound, evidence-based policy responses to enhance security for women around the globe.

"Femicide: A Global Problem — Research Note 14," Small Arms Survey.

false accusations. But the low conviction rate is not evidence of that— it's evidence of how poor our judicial system is as a whole. Survivors of rape, by law, are only allowed to have access to public prosecutors while the accused can hire the best counsel. It takes three months for evidence to come back from a rape kit test.

Three months minimum. Often people will pull out of cases, out of distress due to the drawn out nature of cases.

And what would you, or do you say in response to these arguments?

I would like these people to experience the process of a rape case to see how much a woman has to endure after the brutality she has already been through. Filing a case is an arduous, cumbersome process involving multiple visits to hospitals, police stations, courtrooms—that takes on average two to three years.

And at every stage they are treated terribly. Each time we go to the hospital it takes three hours for someone in the hospital to touch a victim. Even the case I am handling of a child being raped, she had to wait hours to get medical attention.

I would also say, let's discuss solutions and safeguards to put into the law. We all want systematic dispensing of law. So we must have strict provisions in place against false or frivolous complaints.

Perhaps for example, put the burden of proof on the wife as opposed to the husband. Insist that the accused is "Innocent until proven guilty." Maybe make it a bailable offense as opposed to the husband being arrested right away and not getting bail at all.

Or ensure that the conviction would come through expert testimony—from doctors that provide evidence of brutality on the body. Or via prolonged medical history and police reports where you can substantiate sustained periods of violence against the woman. It would not be hard to prove these things through robust evidence.

What's the best way to make progress?

Engaging in uncomfortable conversation around the issue with men. When you lay out simply the level of systematic abuse and discrimination that women experience every day, they tend to understand. Just like when I came to Global Citizen and asked the men in the room if they ever changed their clothes to protect themselves from stares, to help them feel safer wherever they were going, and they all said no. And then every single woman put her hand up in response to the same question.

The most surprising thing I've noticed is that these young men are feeling very marginalized. They feel like they are constantly being looked at as predators. And are not part of the conversation. So it's vital to bring them into it. And help them see they can become champions for the cause.

And when it comes to speaking to women, what issues do you face?

A huge problem in India is that we are not raised as women with the concept of autonomy over our body. Or that sex is something that requires consent from both bodies, that it is done not just for procreation but for pleasure, and not just for the pleasure of a man.

It goes back to this concept of subservience where women can't claim their sexual agency, and that they cannot deny sex to their husband, for sex because it goes against their duty as a wife. I've spoken to women who genuinely don't feel like they can have a say on when they have sex with their husbands or when they don't want to have sex with their husbands.

People genuinely can't grasp their head around the idea, "How can your husband rape you? Does that mean you're not having sex with him? Perhaps if you were satisfying him enough he wouldn't feel the need to demand sex from you?"

In a country where violence within homes is such a taboo subject, how can you even address the issue when women are uncomfortable to come forward and say it's my husband who is raping me? Women within marriages still don't feel like they can come forward and seek help because their support networks discourage it. Parents of women are simply telling them to "Adjust. You are not special. I am being raped, your father rapes me—we just don't call it rape."

Plus there are other factors such as women's financial reliance on their husbands. Or even simply the issue of awareness—many women, especially the younger population do not realise that should they get married and their rapist be their own husband, he will not be punished by law. It will not even be grounds for divorce.

How has your work affected you? Or does it affect you?

It definitely affects me. I would be lying if I said it didn't. I cannot talk to friends because legally I can't share cases. But I encourage everyone on my team to go to counsellors and I go myself from time to time.

Sadly in response to the repeated exposure I have had to the fact that if bad things happen to you as a woman, the system does not help you, I have changed my behavior a lot. I have adopted these defense mechanisms—I will not really go out and feel comfortable partying, or relax in public places. I am very careful all the time.

What keeps you going?

Amongst my team, we have a strong sense of solidarity—when they show up the next day, you show up the next day. Whether it be to the police station, or the hospital, or the courtroom, we show up.

I often say our generation doesn't have another option other than resilience. And I will not stop until this problem is fixed. It may never get fixed. And in that case, I will never stop.

If you had to sum up why you do what you do, what would you say?

When we work in schools and colleges, at the end of a 45-minute session we have on average four to five children, at least, saying they have been abused. These children will come up and say "I now want to report what happened to me as I realize that he has access to other children."

These are children whose parents let them down, for whom everyone around them is saying "just adjust." But these children, after a 45-minute session with us felt comfortable enough to share their stories of abuse. And ask "What can I do to end the cycle of violence?"

So that is always extremely gratifying and reminds me that it will be young people that will lead change in all aspects of life.

What are your hopes for the future?

First, we need comprehensive sex education in all schools. Concepts of consent need to be taught and we need to have open conversations about sex.

Second, we need media to help change the conversation. We have a few popular social media outlets who have addressed the issue briefly. But beyond that there has been little to help push it into mainstream dialogue. We currently have a movie that is being banned by the censorship board in part because it tackles marital rape. We need films that reflect the reality that over 94% of all rapes are committed by someone you know in India—the rapist in films cannot always be someone you don't know.

And of course, I would like to see the law changed. Not simply for future generations, but for my own. I have to get married, then it's my rights in question.

Dowry Demands Constitute Domestic Violence

Virtual Knowledge Centre to End Violence against Women and Girls

In the following viewpoint, writers from the United Nations Entity for Gender Equality and the Empowerment of Women describe dowry-related violence against women around the world. The organization further describes violence against women as related to domestic violence in marriage. Furthermore, the viewpoint showcases legal definitions of "domestic violence" in multiple countries and makes recommendations for legislation that can be passed to minimize intimate partner violence. The viewpoint also details issues regarding the burden of proof when prosecuting dowry-related violence.

As you read, consider the following questions:

1. How does the concept of "economic abuse" relate to violence against women?
2. How does the U.K. currently define "domestic violence," and is it a comprehensive enough definition?
3. What are some of the problems of proof that prosecutors face when proving dowry-related violence?

The violence and deaths associated with dowry demands constitute domestic violence. Similar to acts of domestic violence, the acts used in dowry-related offenses include physical,

"Definition of Dowry-related Violence," Virtual Knowledge Centre to End Violence against Women and Girls, UN Women. Reprinted by permission.

emotional, and economic violence, as well as harassment as means to exact compliance or to punish the victim. Victims will be best served when protected by an expansive domestic violence legislative framework that encompasses dowry-related violence. Drafters should define the scope of prohibited acts within a domestic violence framework, taking into account the dynamics of dowry-related violence. Lawmakers should include violence and harassment related to dowry demands in a definition of domestic violence. Demands for dowry should not be a requisite element in domestic violence laws, however, because of their subtle and often implicit nature.

Example: India's civil law, Protection of Women from Domestic Violence Act, includes dowry-related harassment as a form of domestic violence (Section 3(b)). It is important dowry-related violence and deaths be prohibited under criminal laws, as well. (See Harmful Practices against Women in India: An Examination of Selected Legislative Responses, p. 10.) The Protection of Women From Domestic Violence Act (2005) of India defines domestic violence as follows:

3. Definition of domestic violence.-For the purposes of this Act, any act, omission or commission or conduct of the respondent shall constitute domestic violence in case it -

> (a) harms or injures or endangers the health, safety, life, limb or well-being, whether mental or physical, of the aggrieved person or tends to do so and includes causing physical abuse, sexual abuse, verbal and emotional abuse and economic abuse; or

> (b) harasses, harms, injures or endangers the aggrieved person with a view to coerce her or any other person related to her to meet any unlawful demand for any dowry or other property or valuable security; or

> (c) has the effect of threatening the aggrieved person or any person related to her by any conduct mentioned in clause (a) or clause (b); or

(d) otherwise injures or causes harm, whether physical or mental, to the aggrieved person.

Explanation I.-For the purposes of this section,-

(i) "physical abuse" means any act or conduct which is of such a nature as to cause bodily pain, harm, or danger to life, limb, or health or impair the health or development of the aggrieved person and includes assault, criminal intimidation and criminal force;

(ii) "sexual abuse" includes any conduct of a sexual nature that abuses, humiliates, degrades or otherwise violates the dignity of woman;

(iii) "verbal and emotional abuse" includes

(a) insults, ridicule, humiliation, name calling and insults or ridicule specially with regard to not having a child or a male child; and

(b) repeated threats to cause physical pain to any person in whom the aggrieved person is interested.

(iv) "economic abuse" includes-

(a) deprivation of all or any economic or financial resources to which the aggrieved person is entitled under any law or custom whether payable under an order of a court or otherwise or which the aggrieved person requires out of necessity including, but not limited to, household necessities for the aggrieved person and her children, if any, stridhan, property, jointly or separately owned by the aggrieved person, payment of rental related to the shared household and maintenance;

(b) disposal of household effects, any alienation of assets whether movable or immovable, valuables, shares, securities, bonds and the like or other property in which the aggrieved person has an interest or is entitled to use by virtue of the domestic relationship or which may be reasonably required by the aggrieved person or her children or her stridhan or any other property jointly or separately held by the aggrieved person; and

(c) prohibition or restriction to continued access to resources or facilities which the aggrieved person is entitled to use or enjoy by virtue of the domestic relationship including access to the shared household.

Explanation II.-For the purpose of determining whether any act, omission, commission or conduct of the respondent constitutes "domestic violence" under this section, the overall facts and circumstances of the case shall be taken into consideration. Chapter II, 3

In 2008, a group of experts at meetings convened by the United Nations recommended that "It is therefore essential that any definition of domestic violence that includes psychological and/or economic violence is enforced in a gender-sensitive and appropriate manner. The expertise of relevant professionals, including psychologists and counselors, advocates and service providers for complainants/survivors of violence, and academics should be utilized to determine whether behavior constitutes violence." (See: UN Handbook, 3.4.2; and UN Model Framework, II 3, which urges States to adopt a broad definition of the acts of domestic violence, in compatibility with international standards; and Gender-Based Violence Laws in Sub-Saharan Africa, (2007), p. 52) In 2008, United Nations experts recommended that the definition of domestic violence include economic violence as well as physical, psychological and sexual violence. See: United Nations Handbook for legislation against women, p. 25. The group of experts issued a caveat that by including psychological and economic violence in the definition of domestic violence, drafters and legislators may be creating opportunities for perpetrators to counter-claim psychological or economic abuse against those to whom they are violent. For example, a disgruntled violent abuser may seek protection measures against his wife for using property owned by him. Placing physical abuse on par with economic abuse may lead a perpetrator to claim that physical violence is an appropriate response to an act he sees as economically disadvantageous to him. In the case of dowry-related violence, the husband may argue that the failure to meet dowry remands, such as funds for a family business or the household, constitutes economic abuse against him. Claims of psychological and economic violence may be very difficult to prove in legal proceedings, as well.

Therefore, it is recommended that drafters replace the terms psychological and economic violence with the term coercive control. "Coercive control" includes psychological and economic violence but does so in a way that links the concepts to a pattern of domination through intimidation, isolation, degradation, and deprivation as well as physical assault. The abuser's tactics may include controlling how the victim dresses, cleans, cooks, or performs sexually. These types of extreme control measures target the victim's autonomy, independence and dignity in ways that compromise her ability to make decisions to escape from the subjugation. Therefore, by substituting the term "coercive control" for "psychological violence" and "economic violence" states can target truly harmful behavior and avoid the unintended consequence of turning an imprecise definition of violence against the true victim.

Coercive control is defined as an act or pattern of acts of assault, sexual coercion, threats, humiliation, and intimidation or other abuse that is used to harm, punish or frighten a victim. This control includes a range of acts designed to make victims subordinate and/or dependent by isolating them from sources of support, exploiting their resources and capacities for personal gain, depriving them of the means needed for independence, resistance and escape and regulating their everyday behavior.

Drafters can also draw upon the definition of economic violence from the Violence Prevention Alliance of the World Health

Organization defines violence as "the intentional use of physical force or power, threatened or actual, against oneself, another person, or against a group or community, that either results in or has a high likelihood of resulting in injury, death, psychological harm, maldevelopment, or deprivation." Drafters should focus the definition of economic violence on the intentional use of power, whether threatened or actual, that results in or is likely to result in maldevelopment or deprivation of another person. Drafters should issue legal commentary clarifying that economic deprivation applies to those staples necessary for an adequate standard of living, such as adequate food, clothing and housing, but not material goods nor unsatisfied dowry demands. Drafters may wish to specify in dowry-related domestic violence laws that economic deprivation for dowry-related violence purposes is defined as that aimed at women and girls (See: Article 4(1), CEDAW). The implementation of such legislation that includes the broader definition of domestic violence should be carefully monitored for abuse of process or retributive counterclaims, and if such abuse occurs, the law should be amended. See: Monitoring of Laws on Violence against Women and Girls.

Drafters should carefully consider the types of violence described in the statutory definition. Many experts believe that the definition should include all acts of physical, psychological and sexual abuse between family and household members or intimate partners, as well as in-laws. Drafters should take into account the specific forms of violence perpetrators use in dowry-related crimes and deaths. For example, offenders may use violence disguised as suicides or accidents, such as stove or kerosene disasters, to burn or kill women for failing to meet dowry demands. (See: Shahnaz Bokhari, Good practices in legislation to address harmful practices against women in Pakistan, at 9) They may use acid attacks. Offenders may also use more insidious means to demand dowry, such as starvation, deprivation of clothing, evictions, and false imprisonment. They may subject the woman to forced labor as additional pressure or punishment for failure to meet dowry demands. In addition, drafters should ensure that other acts common in these cases, such as extortion, constitute criminal offenses when they occur between a woman/her family and her groom/fiancée/in-laws.

If a domestic violence law contains a detailed description of prohibited behaviors, it may limit judicial bias. (See: Domestic Violence Legislation and its Implementation: An Analysis for ASEAN Countries Based on International Standards and Good Practices, UNIFEM, June 2009) Drafters should consider, however, that when a detailed list of acts of abuse is included in legislation, it may also have the effect of excluding some unanticipated abusive behavior from legal sanctions. If drafters choose to list forms of violence, the law should specify that the list is not inclusive of all forms of violence.

Legislation should include the following provision in a definition of domestic violence: "No marriage or other relationship shall constitute a defence to a charge of sexual domestic violence under this legislation." (See: UN Handbook, 3.4.3.1)

Drafters should consider including a definition of domestic violence as a course of conduct. For example, The Domestic Violence Act (2007) of Sierra Leone (hereinafter the law of Sierra Leone) contains the following provision:

4. (1) A single act may amount to domestic violence.

(2) A number of acts that form a pattern of behaviour may amount to domestic violence even though some or all of the acts when viewed in isolation may appear minor or trivial. Part II 4

(See: the Combating of Domestic Violence Act (2003) of Namibia (hereinafter law of Namibia) Part I 2 (3) and (4))

Example: the UK recently amended its definition of domestic violence to include coercive control. Domestic violence is now defined as:

"any incident or pattern of incidents of controlling, coercive, threatening behaviour, violence or abuse between those aged 16 or over who are, or have been, intimate partners or family members regardless of gender or sexuality. The abuse can encompass, but is not limited to:

- psychological

- physical

- sexual

- financial

- emotional"

Controlling behavior is defined as "a range of acts designed to make a person subordinate and/or dependent by isolating them from sources of support, exploiting their resources and capacities for personal gain, depriving them of the means needed for independence, resistance and escape and regulating their everyday behaviour." Coercive behavior (non-legal definition) is recognized as "an act or a pattern of acts of assault, threats, humiliation and intimidation or other abuse that is used to harm, punish, or frighten their victim."

(See: UK Home Office, Domestic Violence and Abuse, March 26, 2013)

Legislation should include certain acts which have only recently come to be recognized as serious threats to the complainant/survivor, and which may not be included in criminal law provisions, such as stalking, sometimes called harassment, and acts involving the latest forms of technology. (See: Domestic Violence; Stalking, StopVAW, The Advocates for Human Rights; Bortel, Angela, "Technology and Violence against Women," StopVAW, The Advocates for Human Rights; Minnesota, USA Statute 609.749; Lemon, Nancy K.D., "Domestic Violence and Stalking: A Comment on the Model Anti-Stalking Code Proposed by the National Institute of Justice (1994); and Minnesota Coalition for Battered Women, "Facts About Intimate Partner Stalking in Minnesota and the United States" (2009))

Defining Dowry-related Violence and Dowry

Legislation should provide a definition for dowry-related violence. The UN DAW Expert Group Meeting defines dowry-related violence or harassment as "any act of violence or harassment associated with the giving or receiving of dowry at any time before, during or after the marriage." (See: Good Practices in Legislation on "Harmful Practices" Against Women, Section 3.3.4.1)

Laws should expansively define dowry in terms of its form and when it is demanded, given or received. Dowry should include gifts, money, goods or property given from the bride/wife's family to the groom/husband/in-laws before, during or anytime after the marriage. Laws should frame dowry expansively as a response to explicit or implicit demands or expectations. Laws should omit reference to "in connection with" or "in consideration of" the marriage, to ensure the scope includes all dowry demands whether explicitly connected to the marriage or not.

For example, the following definition will likely prove problematic as it may pose problems of proof. The Parliament of Bangladesh defines dowry as "money, goods or any property which has been given or agreed to give to the bride-groom or his father or mother or any person on his behalf, directly or indirectly, at the time of marriage or before marriage at any time after marriage in condition with the smooth continuation of marital life or as a consideration given by the side of the bride and the money, goods or property which has been demanded from the bride or her father or mother or any person on her behalf, by the bride-groom or his father or mother or any other person on his behalf as the above mentioned condition or consideration." (See: Prevention of Oppression of Women and Children Act (2000), Parliament of Bangladesh, Art. 2(j) (unofficial translation)) Laws should not require dowry be given as a condition for the smooth continuation of marital life or as consideration. Such a requirement may prove challenging to prove because of the covert or implicit nature of dowry demands and expectations.

India defines dowry as:

"any property or valuable security given or agreed to be given either directly or indirectly-

> (a) by one party to a marriage to the other party to the marriage; or

> (b) by the parents of either party to a marriage or by any other person, to either party to the marriage or to any other person; at or before [or any time after the marriage] [in connection with the marriage of the said parties, but does not include] dower or mahr in the case of persons to whom the Muslim Personal Law (Shariat) applies.

In Asia and Africa, There Is a "Missing Women" Problem

Debraj Ray

In the following viewpoint, Debraj Ray details the history of the concept of "missing women," as coined by Amartya Sen, an Indian economist and philosopher who serves as a Professor of Economics and Philosophy at Harvard University. Sen's research computed the number of women who should have been birthed in developed countries in Asia, and the history of the phenomenon. Also in the viewpoint Ray describes how the "unmarriage bias" impacts the rates of missing women around the world. Ray is Silver Professor in the Faculty of Arts and Science and Professor of Economics at New York University.

As you read, consider the following questions:

1. How many women around the world are demographically "missing," and in which countries does this disparity make the most impact?
2. What is the concept of "unmarriage" and why is it prevalent in Asian and African countries?
3. How will these "missing women" impact the birthrates of future generations?

The phrase "missing women," coined by Amartya Sen (1990, 1992), refers to the observation that in parts of the developing world—notably in India and China—the ratio of women to men

"Where Are All the Women?" by Debraj Ray, World Economic Forum, October 19, 2015. Reprinted by permission.

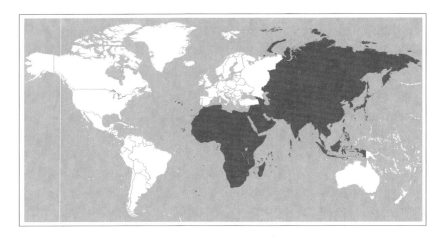

is suspiciously low. On average in developed countries, males outnumber females at birth, but that imbalance begins to redress itself soon after. The combined effect is (or should be) a roughly equal proportion of men and women in the population as a whole. This is not the case in many parts of the developing world.

Sen calculated how skewed sex ratios translate into absolute numbers of missing women. His computations permit us to derive the number of additional women who would have been alive in, say, China or India if these countries had the same ratio of women to men as in developed countries, where women and men presumably receive similar care. Sen's methodology suggests that more than 200 million women are "demographically" missing across the developing world. This is meant to be an estimate of the total number of women who have died prematurely due to gender discrimination.

These astronomical numbers have spawned a significant literature aimed at explaining the "missing women" phenomenon. A central focus of this literature is on skewed sex ratios at birth, a red flag for sex-selective abortion (Junhong 2001, Lin et al. 2014, and Jha et al. 2006). A second area of focus is early childhood and the possibility that young girls are systematically less cared for (Deaton 1989, Garg and Morduch 1998, Oster 2009). Das Gupta (2005) quite fairly summarizises the literature when she states that "the evidence indicates that parental preferences overwhelmingly shape the female deficit in South and East Asia."

In earlier work (Anderson and Ray 2010, 2012), we critically examine the age distribution of missing women. Instead of relying on overall sex ratios that point to an overall "stock" of missing women and make it difficult to separate the problem across different age groups, we use "flow" mortality rates by age and gender. This allows us to estimate the number of missing women (per year) in each age category. In stark contrast to the emphasis in the earlier literature on sex-selective abortion and female infanticide, we found that the vast majority of missing women are actually of adult age. Moreover, a large number of missing adult women are to be found in sub-Saharan Africa, where an unusual birth ratio (the percentage of girls born is biologically higher among African ethnicities) masks the problem from the traditional "stock" viewpoint.

That the majority of missing women are of adult age suggests that excess female mortality across the developing world is not just the result of gender-biased parental preferences. Rather, our estimates reveal that the plight of adult women can be as serious a problem as that of young girls who were either never born or die prematurely in childhood.

In recent work, we take these findings a step further, by examining the role of widowhood in explaining missing women of adult age (Anderson and Ray 2015). There are prima facie reasons for entertaining such a suspicion: that unmarried individuals die at a faster rate than married individuals is well documented. In developed countries, this relative excess mortality for the unmarried occurs at all ages, for both sexes, for all ethnicities, and for all causes of death (Johnson et. al. 2000). While data for developing countries are somewhat coarser, the evidence similarly indicates relative excess mortality for the unmarried in most age groups and for both sexes. Most of this stems from widow(er) hood, given that marriage at a young age is essentially universal in developing countries, so that unmarried adults are typically widowed. None of this is surprising: after all, marriage provides significant economic, psychological and environmental benefits, and it involves two partners caring for each other.

However, the fact that both developed and developing countries suffer from the "unmarriage bias" raises a subtle question about missing women on this particular account. Higher female death rates per se do not imply missing women: these rates relative to those for men must be higher in developing countries. But that isn't a far-fetched possibility: after all, the price of widowhood is particularly steep for women in developing countries. In South Asia, such marginalizisation is well documented for both India and Bangladesh (Chen and Dreze 1992, Jensen 2005, Rahman et al 1992). That vulnerability is not only a result of losing the main breadwinner of the household (the husband), but also of property ownership laws and employment norms which restrict the access of widows to economic resources. Patrilocal norms exacerbate the situation. The economic and social support that a widow receives in her late husband's village is typically extremely limited. Add to these a variety of customs and beliefs:: seclusion and confinement from family and community, a permanent change of diet and dress, discouragement of remarriage, and the fact that often, widows in South Asia are considered bad luck and to be avoided (they are unwelcome at social events, ceremonies and rituals). Moreover, this is a problem on a grand scale: in India, there are more than 40 million widows.

A similar plight can be documented for African countries (Sossou 2002, Oppong 2006). As in South Asia, rules of inheritance and property rights restrict the access of a widow to her late husband's resources. The general isolation of widows (as well as particular rituals of seclusion) is a widespread practice. Widows can be accused of witchcraft and persecuted if they are suspected to have somehow caused their husbands' death. Witchcraft beliefs are widely held throughout sub-Saharan Africa and elderly women are the typical targets of witch killings (Miguel 2005). Customarily, causes for any death are sought within the prevailing social system, and suspected witches in the family of the dead or sick are a prime focus of blame (Oppong 2006).

In short, given these extreme vulnerabilities faced by widows in developing countries, we expect that "excess unmarried mortality" will be relatively more extreme for women in these regions. That sets up the possibility that "unmarriage" alone might explain a significant proportion of the overall numbers of missing women. Now, there are approximately 1.5 million missing women of adult age (20-65) each year. They are distributed over India (and South Asia more generally), China, Southeast and West Asia, and over diverse regions in the African continent. Our methodology indicates that that over 40% of these missing women of adult age can be attributed to not being married. These estimates vary by region. In India and other parts of South and Southeast Asia, roughly 55% of the missing adult women are due to not having a husband. For sub-Saharan Africa, the estimates are somewhat smaller at around 35%, and for China only 13%.

The total number of missing unmarried women each year, by region, are listed in the table below.

DEVELOPING REGION	MISSING WOMEN (AGED 20-65)	UNMARRIED MISSING WOMEN	% DUE TO UNMARRIAGE
Asia:			
India	378,000	184,000	49%
Southeast Asia	86,000	82,000	95%
South Asia	134,000	60,000	45%
China	242,000	31,000	13%
West Asia	17,000	9,000	53%
Africa:			
East Africa	309,000	119,000	38%
West Africa	210,000	58,000	28%
Southern Africa	69,000	31,000	45%
Central Africa	82,000	28,000	34%
North Africa	35,000	19,000	54%
TOTAL:	**1,562,000**	**622,000**	**40%**

DATA Sources: United Nations.UN World Marriage Data 2012; UN Demographic Yearbook 2003; UN World Population Prospects: The 2012 Revision.

Approximately 70% of the missing unmarried women are of reproductive age (20-45). These younger unmarried women are classified as missing precisely because in Asia and Africa, their death rates relative to those for unmarried men are extremely high compared to the same ratio in benchmark developed countries. The significant discrepancy stems from limited access to resources and health care for this very socially marginalizised group.

The remaining 30% of the missing unmarried women are older (between 45 and 65). Our computations demonstrate that excess female mortality amongst this older unmarried group is driven mainly by a second key factor: the relative incidence of widowhood is larger in developing regions. It may well be that this factor is not as directly linked to gender discrimination, and has more to do with patterns of mortality across age and gender with development. But further research is needed to identify precisely the sources of the significant excess female mortality from the absence of marriage amongst women in parts of Asia and Africa.

The vulnerabilities faced by unmarried women in developing countries have been much discussed. Our approach places these vulnerabilities explicitly in the context of missing women, thus permitting a comparison across different sources of excess female mortality. The resulting statistic—that over 40% of excess female mortality can be attributed to just this one factor—is quite remarkable.

Periodical and Internet Sources Bibliography

The following articles have been selected to supplement the diverse views presented in this chapter.

Christina Asquith, "This Week in Women: Violence Against Women Hurts Communities Around the World," *Ms. Magazine*, April 13, 2018. http://msmagazine.com/blog/2018/04/13/week-women-violence-women-hurts-communities-around-world/.

BWW News Desk, "World Premiere of #JustMen Tackles Violence Against Women and Children at the Baxter," Broadway World South Africa, May 25, 2018. https://www.broadwayworld.com/south-africa/article/World-Premiere-Of-JustMen-Tackles-Violence-Against-Women-And-Children-At-The-Baxter-20180525.

Archana Chaudhary, Saritha Rai, Dhwani Pandya, "Sexual Violence Is Holding Back the Rise of India," *Bloomberg*, May 28, 2018. https://www.bloomberg.com/news/features/2018-05-28/sexual-violence-is-holding-back-the-rise-of-india.

Amanda Dale, "To Counter Domestic Homicide, Tighten Gun Control," TheStar.com, June 2, 2018. https://www.thestar.com/opinion/contributors/2018/06/02/to-counter-domestic-homicide-tighten-gun-control.html.

Melissa Davey, "Online Sexism Targeted in World-First 'Bystander' Project," *Guardian,* May 31, 2018. https://www.theguardian.com/world/2018/jun/01/online-sexism-targeted-in-world-first-bystander-project.

Karen Feldscher, "Reframing Gender Violence as a Preventable Disease," Harvard School of Public Health, May 24, 2018. https://www.hsph.harvard.edu/news/features/student-profile-alice-han-gender-violence/.

Melanie McFarland, "We All Live in "Dietland": This Revenge Fantasy Takes on Violence Against Women in All Forms," Salon, June 2, 2018. https://www.salon.com/2018/06/02/we-all-live-in-dietland-this-revenge-fantasy-takes-on-violence-against-women-in-all-forms/.

Rebecca Omonira-Yoekanmi, "Feminist Journalists Must Document Structural Violence Against Women—With Investigations from Below," Open Democracy, May 31, 2018. https://www.opendemocracy.net/5050/rebecca-omonira-oyekanmi/feminist-anti-racist-investigations-from-below.

Paul Solman, "Why the New Global Wealth of Educated Women Spurs Backlash," PBS, May 31, 2018. https://www.pbs.org/newshour/show/why-the-new-global-wealth-of-educated-women-spurs-backlash.

UN Women, "Facts and Figures: Ending Violence Against Women," UN Women, August 2017. http://www.unwomen.org/en/what-we-do/ending-violence-against-women/facts-and-figures.

Rachel Vogelstein, "Why #JusticeForNoura Matters," Council on Foreign Relations, June 1, 2018. https://www.cfr.org/blog/why-justicefornoura-matters.

Vivian Wang, "The #MeToo Movement Came to Albany. But Will It Stick?," *New York Times*, June 1, 2018. https://www.nytimes.com/2018/06/01/nyregion/metoo-albany-sexual-harassment.html.

GLOBALVIEWPOINTS

CHAPTER 2

Societal Causes and Effects of Violence Against Women

In the United States African American Women Are More Likely to Be Victims of Domestic Violence

Institute on Domestic Violence in the African American Community

In the following excerpted viewpoint, writers from the Institute on Domestic Violence in the African American Community describe domesic violence as specifically focused on African American women, in which the rates of violence are significantly higher than the rates of violence against white women. The viewpoint describes the manners in which domestic violence is caused and points out that over 6,400 women were murdered by an intimate partner using a gun between the years of 2001 and 2012, and how most African American murder victims, whether it is domestic violence or not, are murdered with a firearm. The Institute on Domestic Violence in the African American Community is an organization dedicated to understanding and ending violence in the African American community.

As you read, consider the following questions:

1. How does the marginalization of African American women correlate with the high rates of domestic violence that this group faces?
2. Why is context crucial when researching the domestic violence faced by African American women?
3. Why is maternal homicide involving minority women underreported and underpublicized?

"Facts about Domestic Violence & African American Women," Institute on Domestic Violence in the African American Community (IVAAC). Reprinted by permission.

The public health consequences of intimate partner violence of African American women in the USA are significant. In addition, emotional and physical trauma can result in depression, anxiety, suicide, post-traumatic stress disorder, and even homicide. Many Black women experience lost productivity due to feelings of shame, difficulty focusing, eating disorders, inability to care for their children, engaging in high risk behaviors, substance abuse, and developing chronic health problems. There are feelings of isolation and distrust of others, and this often impacts a woman's ability for seeking help.

Statistics from the American Bar Association's Commission on Domestic Violence found that Black females experienced intimate partner violence at a rate 35% higher than that of White females, and about 22 times the rate of women of other races (Rennison & Welchans, 2000). The ABA Commission also found that African American women experience more domestic violence than White women in the age group of 20-24 years old. African American women who are marginalized, such as low-income dating teens, pregnant women, and older adult women are at tremendous risk for victimization by an intimate partner. The data on racial disparities in intimate partner violence, including femicide, have remained fairly consistent for more than a decade. It is for these reasons that this series of fact sheets will focus on: Realities of Black Women's Lives: Social Determinants of Domestic Violence.

Our intent is to provide fact sheets including quantitative data and research findings about the impact of domestic violence on Black Women. We are seeking to document current factual trends and highlight the voices of African American victims on various intersections of domestic violence. Specific components will focus on: trauma, homicide, health factors, child maltreatment, teen dating violence, HIV/AIDS, and returning home from incarceration or parole. It is well documented that race or ethnicity, sex, sexual orientation, gender identity, age, disability, socioeconomic status, and geographic location all contribute to an individual's vulnerability to be a victim of all forms of violence. It is important to recognize the impact that these social determinants can have to produce negative outcomes for African American women, children and teens. In other words, health disparities often adversely affect groups of people who have experienced greater obstacles to achieving healthy outcomes.

An important first step is to have an understanding and awareness of the problem. The Centers for Disease Control (CDC) and Prevention defines domestic violence as a pattern of behavior which involves violence or other abuse by one person against another in a domestic status, such as being in an intimate partner relationship. This could involve couples that are heterosexual or in same sex relationships. The violence can be physical, emotional, verbal, economic or sexual abuse, which can range from subtle, coercive forms to marital rape and to violent physical abuse that results in disfigurement or death. The term domestic violence is interchangeable with domestic abuse, spousal abuse, battering, family violence and intimate partner violence.

Steering Committee members of the Institute on Domestic Violence in the African American Community (IDVAAC) are committed to the prevention of violence against women and are responsible for the development of this series of fact sheets.

[...]

Black homicide in the United States remains at an alarming level. Black femicide, the homicide of Black women, is the leading cause of death among young Black women age 15 to 34 and is one of the leading causes of premature death among Black women overall. Government reports as well as scholarly research have substantiated that African Americans experience disproportionate homicide victimization; as compared with their White counterparts, Black women are three times more likely to be murdered (Langley & Sugarmann, 2014). Black women are three times more likely to die at the hands of a partner or ex-partner than members of other racial groups. In the majority of cases, their perpetrators were intimate partners.

The contextual aspects of Black female homicide victimization are important. For Black female homicides (in which there was sufficient law enforcement reporting about the victim-offender relationship and about the circumstances surrounding the fatality) most perpetrators were intimate partners or ex-partners. A history of prior physical abuse, especially near-fatal assaults, is the primary risk factor for intimate partner femicide (Nicolaidis, 2003). Femicide is also highly correlated with coercive controlling violence, defined as a pattern of emotionally abusive intimidation, manipulation, coercion and control that may not necessarily involve physical harm (Kelly & Johnson, 2008). Black femicide often occurs in the context of an argument or around the time of a significant relationship change (e.g., pregnancy, separation).

According to data from the Centers for Disease Control (CDC) and Prevention's National Violent Death Reporting System, expectant mothers are more likely to die from homicide than from obstetric-related causes (Cheng & Horon, 2010). The CDC reports that the probability of being murdered while pregnant or within the year after childbirth is 11 times higher for Black women ages 25-29 than their White counterparts (Palladino et al., 2011). Despite this alarming statistic, cases of maternal homicide involving minority women are underreported and underpublicized (CBSNEWS, CBS April 11, 2008, 11:44 AM). With respect to maternal homicide in the context of domestic violence, the mass media often sensationalizes the murder of White expectant mothers, as in the high profile case of Laci Peterson. Meanwhile, the media pays little attention to similar cases involving Black victims – which are far more prevalent.

The Federal Bureau of Investigation reports that 6,410 women were murdered by an intimate partner using a gun, between 2001 and 2012. The prevalence of firearms in the United States has key implications for the Black community. Most Black murder victims, regardless of sex, are killed with guns. Many women obtain guns for safety reasons; unfortunately, female homicide victims are often killed with the guns that they possess for protection.

According to law enforcement statistics for 2012, Blacks – who comprise only 15 percent of the US Population – represent 51 percent of murder victims (Langley & Sugarmann, 2014). This crime is predominantly intraracial. The murder rate for Black males is 6 times higher than that for Black females. Nonetheless, the murder rate of Black females is significantly higher than that of White females. The homicide victimization of Black women often involves three characteristics:

1. The perpetrator is not a stranger: he is known to the victim, is an intimate partner, or is former partner
2. The murder occurs in the context of a domestic dispute
3. The most common murder weapon is a firearm

In order for law enforcement groups, policymakers, and service providers to develop effective violence prevention and intervention initiatives, they will need to consider this reality.

Narrative

Charlene was an attractive woman in her mid-twenties. She worked in the food service industry and had a modest income. Her less fortunate boyfriend Henry, who was often either underemployed or unemployed, frequently relied on her for financial support. Charlene confided with a close friend about Henry's episodic violent outbursts. She was concerned that his violent behavior had become more frequent and more intense. Nonetheless, Charlene remained in this volatile relationship for a variety of reasons: hope that Henry would change, shame, and fear of retaliation. Like many women, she did not realize how dangerous her situation had become. Charlene belatedly decided to leave Henry. One Friday evening, as she was fleeing her home with suitcase in hand, Henry confronted her. That was Charlene's last night in our community.

Her story is a familiar story. Why do abused women stay? Black women remain in abusive relation-ships for a variety of complex reasons:

- Emotional attachment
- Fear of batterer (retaliation, stalking)
- Financial dependence
- Child custody issues
- Shame
- Anxiety about family and community responses (stigmatization, marginalization)

The absence of effective support systems that might facilitate their leaving as well as limited knowledge of or access to community resources are other important factors.

Facts

- According to a report from the Violence Policy Center (Langley & Sugarmann, 2014:1), in 2011, the homicide rate for Black female victims (4.54 per 100,000) was more than three times higher than the homicide rate for White female victims. (1.45 per 100,000).
- In 2012, for "homicides in which the victim to offender relationship could be identified, 93 percent of female victims (1,487 out of 1,594) were murdered by a male they knew" (Violence Policy Center, 2014: 3).

- The CDC's Pregnancy Mortality Surveillance System (PMSS) shows a significant racial disparity in pregnancy-associated homicides during the 1990s. Comparing the homicides of pregnant White and Black women, the likelihood of being murdered was five times greater for Black women who are younger than 20 years and eleven times greater for Black women who are in the 25 to 29 age bracket (Chang et al., 2005).

- Firearms increase the lethality risk in domestic violence situations. From 1980 to 2008, guns were used to commit two-thirds of intimate partner homicides (Cooper & Smith, 2011). Intimate partner femicide is much more likely to occur in homes where a gun is present.

Recommendations:

1) Build on Best Practices: Risk Assessment and Fatality Review
The Lethality Assessment Program (LAP)

Evaluating the threat posed by situations and individuals has emerged as an important practice for public safety and public health. Lethality Assessment Programs/Protocols (LAPs) are risk assessment tools that provide a simple, consistent measure of a victim's level of danger in a situation. Administered by law enforcement and other first responders, LAPs are designed to prevent the escalation of the intimate partner abuse and encourage help-seeking behavior by the victim. LAPs involve partnerships with law enforcement, domestic violence service agencies, and community-based organizations. In addition to gauging threat levels, these programs provide victims with the counseling and resources needed to formulate safety plans and to evaluate alternatives to staying with abusive partners.

As of 2013, jurisdictions in 31 states have implemented LAPs.

Domestic Violence Fatality Review Teams (DVFRT)

Domestic Violence Fatality Review Teams (DVFRT) are multidisciplinary, interprofessional groups that critique domestic violence homicide cases. DVFRT members usually have expertise in the following areas: public health, public safety, social service delivery, policymaking, and education. Although their structure and procedures may vary significantly, DVFRTs seek to better understand:

- the causes of intimate partner violence
- the personal, situational, and environmental factors that heighten or mitigate the risk for injury and death
- the relative effectiveness of specific prevention measures

Increasing the cultural competence of DVFRTs is essential for these groups to understand issues that are unique to communities of color and to accurately evaluate Black femicide cases.

2) Review and Modify Policies: "Protect and Serve" or Persecute?

With respect to domestic violence, law enforcement and the judicial system have a two-fold responsibility: protect the victims and punish the perpetrators. Unfortunately, lack of coordination between law enforcement entities (e.g., local police and federal authorities) and legal loopholes often allow perpetrators to manipulate systems and victims. Black communities tend to be suspicious of both the police and courts. This distrust is rooted in historic injustices (i.e., segregation, attacks by police during the civil rights movement) and fueled by contemporary controversies (i.e., racial profiling, fatal shootings of unarmed Black men, military-style policing of the protests in Ferguson, Missouri). The routine criminalization and mass incarceration of Black men also contribute to tension between black communities and authorities. In many respects, these problems undermine the efforts of law enforcement and the judicial system to reduce Black intimate partner femicide.

3) Expand Domestic Violence Prevention and Education Initiatives

To increase the effectiveness of violence prevention and education efforts, programs should be targeted and culturally sensitive. Program design and materials need to reflect the age, education level, and culture of various audiences. Due to the increase in dating violence, education about healthy relationships should begin in earlier grades.

Although the challenges seem daunting, collaborations between the law enforcement, the judicial system, health-care providers, social service agencies, and community-based organizations can potentially reduce the intimate partner abuse and killing suffered by Black women.

In Guatemala Women Are Killed for Being Women

Kelsey Alford-Jones

In the following excerpted viewpoint Kelsey Alford-Jones of the Guatemala Human Rights Commission points out the increasing violence in Guatemala, and how women are significantly more impacted by it than women in many other violence-afflicted countries around the world. Not only are the rates of violence against women so high, they are also uncommonly high against young girls, and these cases of sadistic and violent murders are not properly investigated by the authorities, bringing rise to legislation that is attempting to mitigate this situation.

As you read, consider the following questions:

1. In what ways does Guatemala's history of armed conflict correlate with rising levels of violence against women?
2. How have organized crime and gang violence also impacted violence against women in Guatemala?
3. Why is it important to have legislation that protects women? Use examples from the Guatemalan conflict described in the viewpoint.

In Guatemala, women have been targeted simply for being women. This phenomenon has occurred in other regions such as the border town of Ciudad Juárez, Mexico, where there have

"Guatemala' s Femicide Law: Progress Against Impunity?" by Kelsey Alford-Jones, Guatemala Human Rights Commission, May 2009. Reprinted by permission.

PIERCE COLLEGE LIBRARY

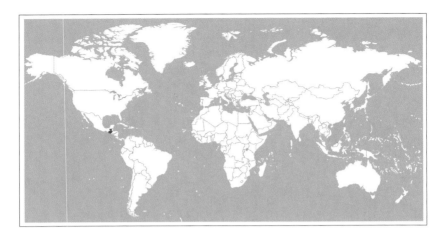

been 400 unsolved cases of brutal murders. In South Africa, there are exceedingly high rates of domestic violence, with one woman killed almost every six hours by her partner. Gaza and North Carolina have also been identified as regions with high rates of violence against women.[2]

This pattern of violence has been termed femicide. Femicide is officially defined as the murder of a woman because of her gender. Femicide is often carried out with shocking brutality; many victims show signs of torture and mutilation.[3]

A contributing factor to the continued crime of Femicide is the absence of state guarantees to protect the rights of women. The term femicide is often accompanied by the political term feminicide. Feminicide holds responsible not only the male perpetrators but also the state and judicial structures that normalize misogyny, tolerate the perpetrators' acts of violence, or deny state responsibility to ensure the safety of its female citizens.[4]

Guatemala suffers from both femicide and feminicide. With a population of fewer than 14 million, the nation registered over 4,000 violent murders of women from 2000 to 2008.[5] An estimated 98% of the cases reported remain in impunity.[6] The stories of Claudina Velásquez and María Isabel Franco are egregious examples of the sadistic and violent murder of young women and have become representative of the thousands of cases that are not properly investigated and are never solved.

Recognizing the increasingly violent conditions faced by women, Guatemalan activists worked to achieve official recognition of femicide. They faced an uphill battle against a long history of violence against women, gender inequality, and the institutionalized acceptance of impunity for offenders. The political will to address the situation was slow to materialize and took years of support and lobbying from women's groups and discussion with the international community—including non-governmental organizations and the US Congress.

Their hard work paid off and on April 9, 2008 when the Guatemalan congress passed Decree 22-2008, the Law Against Femicide and Other Forms of Violence Against Women, officially recognizing femicide as a punishable crime. It also codifies an expansive definition of violence against women.

The Femicide Law represents an important step in stemming the targeted and brutal murder of women, and serves as a model for women's rights activists in other countries. This unique piece of legislation is one step in the struggle for women's right to live in Guatemala. However, much more is needed to fight this battle.

A year has passed since the approval of the law; yet the number of women murdered continues to rise. The most violent year to date for women in Guatemala was 2008 with 722 violent deaths reported and many more cases of abuse. In just the first two weeks of January 2009, 26 women were killed; the number grew to 57 by the end of the month.[7] The process of investigation, prosecution and prevention of murders in Guatemala remains weak or non-existent. Victims' families continue to face persecution, fear, and denial of justice from the state entities responsible for investigation of the murders.

Women's rights advocates continue to push for implementation of the law while lawyers, judges, and victims' families are just beginning to become familiar with the new legislation.

Femicide

"Femicide is on the extreme end of a continuum of antifemale terror that includes a wide variety of verbal and physical abuse, such as rape, torture, sexual slavery(particularly in prostitution), incestuous and extrafamilial child sexual abuse, physical and emotional battery, sexual harassment (on the phone, in the streets, at the office, and in the classroom), genital mutilation (clitoridectomies, excision, infibulations), unnecessary gynecological operations (gratuitous hysterectomies), forced heterosexuality, forced sterilization, forced motherhood (by criminalizing contraception and abortion), psychosurgery, denial of food to women in some cultures, cosmetic surgery, and other mutilations in the name of beautification. Whenever these forms of terrorism result in death, they become femicides."

"Femicide / Feminicide", MuJER.

This report investigates the history and context of femicide in Guatemala, the components of the law, and reactions and recommendations one year later.

Specifically, this report attempts to answer the questions:

- Why does femicide exist in Guatemala?

- Why does the number of women killed continue to rise?

- What has the law accomplished and what is lacking?

Femicide in Context

We must seek a way to heal the wounds in order to combat this culture of violence.

—Alba Maldonado, Congresswoman, URNG[8]

To understand why femicide exists in Guatemala, it is important to understand the historical, cultural and socio-political context of gender inequality, misogyny, and continued corruption and impunity.

A Violent Past

Looking to the past, including Guatemala's 36-year internal armed conflict, sheds light on the current violence against women. The conflict, officially classified as genocide by the United Nations, resulted in the rape, torture, and murder of tens of thousands of Guatemalan women and girls. The war irrevocably damaged the family structure, the community, and the nation.[9] The Guatemalan army, paramilitary (civilian defense patrols) and police used violence against women as a weapon of war.

The rape and torture of women as a military weapon during wartime has been used worldwide. Rape, when used as a weapon of war, is systematically employed for a variety of purposes, including intimidation, humiliation, political terror, extracting information, rewarding soldiers, and "ethnic cleansing."[10] In Guatemala, this form of abuse and torture was used as a counterinsurgency tactic most notably in the early 1980s by the military in the rural highland indigenous regions.[11]

Women are recognized in Guatemala (and many other cultures) as the givers of life, the transmitters of culture and the pillars of the community. Raping, torturing, and killing a woman is a way to destroy not only the individual woman, but to dishonor her family, her community, and her national and ethnic identity. Her honor is destroyed (as well as her emotional, physical, and mental integrity) thus destroying the collective identity and spirit of her family, community, and ethnic group.

The seminal reports on historic and collective memory of the Guatemalan war each have a chapter dedicated to violence against women. The Recovery of Historical Memory project (REHMI) headed by the late Bishop Juan Gerardi of the Archbishop's Human Rights Office includes testimony from thousands of Guatemalan victims, survivors, and witnesses. The report Never Again (1998) documents the brutality directed against the Mayan people and specifically the women.

The Commission for Historical Clarification (CEH), a U.N.-sponsored truth and reconciliation commission ordered under the Oslo Accords of 1994, was created to produce an impartial report on the human rights violations that were committed during the war and make recommendations to encourage peace, preserve the historic memory of victims, and foster mutual respect for human rights. Guatemala: Memory of Silence (1999) was created from thousands of interviews with Guatemalans.[12] The CEH report estimates that 25% (50,000) of the victims of war were women and described rape as "a generalized and systematic practice carried out by State agents as a counterinsurgency strategy... [which] came to constitute a true weapon of terror."[13]

The CEH identified 9,411 female victims of gender violence; of those, 19% were tortured and 14% suffered sexual violence.[14] The victims were primarily adults, although children and the elderly were not exempt; 35% of the victims were under 17 years of age. Sexual violence was routinely implemented during torture or immediately prior to murder, with 25% assassinated after their abuse.[15] The vast majority who suffered sexual violence (88.8%) was Mayan.[16] Women were frequently gang-raped or forced to have sex with soldiers in front of family members; one interview reports 30 men raping a woman and her daughter in Quiché.[17]

Pregnant women in particular were targeted for violence by the Guatemalan military and civilian patrols (PACs). Survivors of the conflict attested to these atrocities, remembering the fetuses that were cut out of womens bodies and even hung on trees.[18]

"Women were seen as war booty that soldiers could make use of as they pleased" states Hilda Morales, a women's rights activist, lawyer, and member of the National Women's Office (ONAM) and the Network against Violence against Women (Red Nacional de Mujeres Contra la Violencia).[19] The REHMI project reported that an act of sexual violence constituted a form of "victory" for the army.[20] Eliminating Mayan women was inextricably linked with that of eliminating the guerrilla, thus "justifying" the extreme acts of violence against women.[21]

The REHMI report, Nunca Más, provides testimony that explains how sexual violations constituted much more than physical acts of violence.[22] The consequences for victims of sexual violence include serious and chronic medical problems, psychological damage, life-threatening diseases, forced pregnancy, infertility, and stigmatization and/or rejection by family members and communities. The women were often forced to live in silence in the same community as their aggressor. Women were blamed for the crimes against them, a tactic used to foster a sense of distrust and skepticism among the general public towards the victims.[23]

Congresswoman Alba Maldonado said it is impossible not to relate the violence during the internal conflict with the current wave of brutal murders of women, given that thousands of men were trained to commit acts of gendered violence and subsequently reintegrated into society.[24] Evidence supports this, as the rise of violence against women in the last decade, including rape, dismemberment, and techniques of torture and mutilation, is reminiscent of tactics used during the war. The wartime practice of stigmatizing and blaming the victim emerges in today's investigative process, whereby many victims are dismissed as prostitutes, gang members, or criminals, unworthy of investigation.

A Culture of Violence: Contributing Social Factors

The suffering endured by women during the internal armed conflict did not end with the signing of the peace accords. Organized crime, gangs, drug trafficking, and human trafficking are part of daily life not only in the capital city, but also throughout the countryside.

Four factors have had a particular influence on women:

- Violence perpetrated by drug trafficking;

- Gang activity;

- A culture of machismo or misogyny that targets women as victims and continues the brutal sexual violence against women;

- A lack of rule of law, including corruption, gender bias and impunity in law enforcement, investigations and the legal system.

[…]

Gangs

Gang violence has risen over the past 15 years in Guatemala; the majority of the estimated 80,000 members belong to the MS-13 Salvatrucha and the M-18 gangs (that originated in Los Angeles). Gang members extort local business owners, bus drivers, local students on their way to school, and other members of society; a portion of this "tax" is spent on weapons.

Gang members include young men and women who are often recruited by force, and threatened with violence and death if they leave the gang, of which they become lifelong members. Gang initiation often includes killing an innocent victim, and several cases of femicide have been linked to this rite of passage. In some instances, female victims garner different levels of "points" for the particular gang.[29]

Kidnapping is higher in Guatemala than in notorious Colombia; women and children are often targets, to extort a ransom from family members. "Express kidnapping" is common in San Marcos, where the kidnapper negotiates a ransom with the family, to release the hostages within hours for a smaller fee.[30]

The social insecurity and violence attributed to gangs is increasingly widespread. Gangs are no longer confined to the cities, but are found in rural areas, indigenous villages, small towns, and small cities including the war torn departments of Quiche, Baja Verapaz, and San Marcos.

Machismo and Misogyny

Societal acceptance and perpetuation of strong gender bias and "machista" attitudes underlies violence against women in Guatemala, on the street, in the home, in the courtroom, and at the scene of the crime. Women are heads of household in increasing numbers (due to abandonment, migration, and other factors) and are forced to work outside the home to provide for their children. Working late, taking public transportation, or walking home late at night increases the risk of becoming a victim of violence. Traditional Guatemalan culture says a woman's place is in the home; if she is attacked on the street, she is blamed for not taking precautions.

Women face potential violence on several fronts. During the war, an army of approximately 40,000 men and a Civilian Defense Unit of approximately one million men were trained to commit acts of gendered violence, both emotional and physical. After the 1996 Peace Accords, these men returned to civil society with no services available to pave the transition from a wartime mentality.[31]

[…]

A Lack of Rule of Law

Impunity in cases of violence against women and femicide is staggeringly high. Dr. Carlos Castresana, Commissioner of the International Commission Against Impunity in Guatemala (CICIG), has identified impunity as the overwhelming factor in the femicide crisis.[36]

Between 2005 and 2007 only 2% of 2,000 cases involving the violent deaths of women were "resolved" (some without convictions).[37] Anabella Noriega of the Human Rights Ombudsman's Office also reported that in 2004 only one case out of 500 resulted in a conviction (a rate of .002%).[38]

Families and victims who denounce crimes against women are often faced with corrupt or indifferent police, strong gender bias, and a dysfunctional judicial system.

Authorities have pinpointed the municipalities most prone to femicides (Mixco, Villa Nueva, Escuintla, Quetzaltenango, and Cobán) and note that the majority of the crimes are committed with a firearm. Yet the Guatemalan National Police force is understaffed, lacks training on how to approach female victims of violence, and is notoriously corrupt.

Despite legislation to the contrary, domestic violence is commonly dismissed as a "private" matter. Police are slow to respond to complaints of violence against women and sometimes fail to appear at all.[39] Norma Cruz, director of the Survivor's Foundation, an organization that provides legal, psychosocial, accompaniment, and shelter services for victims of abuse and their families, recounted one incident in which police refused to enter a home where a husband was beating and threatening his wife so as not to interfere with his rights.[40] "The system does not respond," she stated.

Gender bias permeates the investigative process as well. The Public Prosecutor's Office (MP) is responsible for the investigation of femicide cases.[41] It includes several entities created to protect the rights of women, including the Women's Office (Fiscalía de la Mujer), Office of Human Rights (Fiscalía de Derechos Humanos), and Crimes Against Life and Personal Integrity Unit (Fiscalía de Delitos contra la Vida y la Integridad de la Persona).[42] Despite the numerous offices, gender bias permeates the investigative process, resulting in further impunity.

Despite nominal support for women's rights in these institutions, investigators delay the initial investigation by dismissing the victims as prostitutes, gang members, or criminals. A female victim's physical attire or appearance are often cause for delay or stigmatization, as in the case of Claudina Velásquez who was initially ignored for her belly ring and sandals.[43]

The practice of blaming the victim is most evident in "crimes of passion," a violent death at the hands of a lover or former lover. Both Amnesty International and anthropologist Victoria Sanford report that crimes of passion are rarely investigated, with the female victims regarded as unfaithful and "dishonest" and therefore somewhat responsible for their unfortunate demise.[44]

Hilda Morales and REDNOVI conducted a review of the court system and the implementation of the Domestic Violence Law of 1996. They found that in many cases, authorities simply refused to implement the law that would protect women from domestic violence. Women were viewed as instigating the acts of violence "because they do not cook well, because they do not do their chores, and because they do not obey their husbands."[45]

When perpetrators of violence against women operate in a climate of impunity, there is little incentive to change their behavior.[46] The Human Rights Ombudsman (PDH) has concluded that Guatemala is suffering from a psychological problem at a national level; crimes against women are not recognized, not investigated, and not brought to justice.[47] In the April 2008 report on Femicide in Guatemala, the PDH states, "In Guatemala, only 15% of the bodies are hidden, and the rest are left in a public place or in the victim's home, which indicates that the victimizers are not attempting to hide the crime."

[…]

Protection

Greater protection is needed for women survivors of violence, their children, and the families of femicide victims. Furthermore, each social/ethnic group requires assistance particular to their situation (such as indigenous women, students, housewives, or sex workers). GHRC recommends:

- Increased police forces with specific training for violence against women. The Guatemalan Police force is severely understaffed (currently 19,000 officers, with an estimated 50,000 required to provide adequate security for the population of 14 million). Current police training needs to include awareness, knowledge, and specialized courses on women's rights, how to interact with a female victim and preserve valuable evidence when arriving on the scene of the crime, and a thorough knowledge of victim's rights and emergency services available to survivors.[101]

- Support of alternative models for justice centers. The US funded model 24-hour police and judicial center located in Villa Nueva (Guatemala City) has been more effective in providing services to citizens than the traditional model.

Police officers are stationed every 2-3 blocks in gang neighborhoods to stem extortion and sexual assault of girls.[102]

- Increased protection for civil servants in the judicial sector who are often subject to intimidation and threats.[103]

- Protection for human rights officials and their families. The case of Gladys Monterroso, wife of Sergio Morales, Human Rights Ombudsman, is an example of how women family members are attacked for political purposes and to generate and perpetuate a climate of terror. (Ms. Monterroso was kidnapped, tortured, and raped on March 25, 2009).[104]

- USAID funding for witness protection programs and legal aid to encourage victims and families to speak out against violent crimes and seek justice.[105]

- Expansion of services for women who are victims of violence outside the home. While the CAIMU are an important service, they serve only victims of domestic violence.[106]

[…]

Notes

2. For more on Femicide in other regions of the world, see "Femicides of Juarez Fact Sheet." National Organization for Women. http://www.now.org/issues/global/juarez/femicide.html; Ellis, Estelle. "Dying at the Hands of Their Lovers." *Cape Argus.* http://www.capeargus.co.za/index.php?fSectionId=49&fArticleId=2130110 See also Matthews, Shanaaz, et al. "Intimate Femicide-Suicide in South Africa: A Cross-Sectional Study." *Bulletin of the World Health Organization.* July 2008, 86 (7) http://www.who.int/bulletin/volumes/86/7/07-043786.pdf; "OPT: 'Femicide on the Rise in Conflict Zone.'" *IRIN.* UN Office for the Coordination of Humanitarian Affairs. 7 March 2007. http://www.irinnews.org/Report.aspx?ReportId=70554; Moracco, Kathryn. "Femicide in North Carolina, 1991-1993." *Homicide Studies,* Vol. 2, No. 4, 422-446 (1998). http://hsx.sagepub.com/cgi/content/abstract/2/4/422

3. See Radford, Jill, and Diane E. H. Russell, (eds.) F*emicide: The Politics of Woman Killing.* New York: Twayne Publishers, 1992, 6-7. For a summary of the text, see Sunshine for Women. Book Summaries. http://www.pinn.net/~sunshine/book-sum/femicide.html For information on Diane Russell, see "Femicide." http://www.dianarussell.com/femicide.html Russell coined the term "femicide" in the early 1990s. though both "femicide" and "feminicide" are used to describe violence against women. For the purpose of this report, the term "femicide" will be used as it appears in the written law. For a comprehensive study, see Grupo de Apoyo Mutuo (GAM). "Guatemala 1999-2006: Origin, manifestación, y

tendencias del feminicidio." *Feminicio* 2007. http://www.gam.org.gt/public/publi/pdf/feminicidio%202007.pdf See also Sanford, Victoria. "From Genocide to Feminicide: Impunity and Human Rights in Twenty-first Century Guatemala." *Journal of Human Rights,* 7:104-122, 2008. Routledge, Taylor and Francis Group. http://johnjay.cuny.edu/From_Genocide_to_Feminicide.pdf

4. Though both "femicide" and "feminicide" are used to describe violence against women, for the purpose of this report, the term "femicide" will be used as it appears in the written law. For a comprehensive study, see Grupo de Apoyo Mutuo (GAM). "Guatemala 1999-2006: Origin, manifestación, y tendencias del feminicidio." *Feminicidio* 2007. http://www.gam.org.gt/public/publi/pdf/feminicidio%202007.pdf See also Sanford, Victoria. "From Genocide to Feminicide: Impunity and Human Rights in Twenty-first Century Guatemala." *Journal of Human Rights,* 7:104-122, 2008. Routledge, Taylor and Francis Group. http://johnjay.cuny.edu/From_Genocide_to_Feminicide.pdf

5. "Informe Anual Circunstanciado Resumen Ejecutivo 2008." Procurador de los Derechos Humanos. Guatemala, 2009. p 179-180; Fundación Sobrevivientes cited in "Norma Cruz y el derecho de la mujer; años de lucha por dignidad," Prensa Libre 1 February 2009. http://www.prensalibre.com/pl/2009/febrero/01/290913.html

6. Orantes, Coralia. "Cicig ve impunidad en casos de femicidio." Nacional. *Prensa Libre.* 23 May 2008. http://www.prensalibre.com/pl/2008/mayo/23/239895.html

7. Norma Cruz, email to the author, 23 February 2009. See also Castillo, Juan Manuel. "Veintiséis mujeres mueren de forma violenta en 16 días." País. *El Periódico.* 17 January 2009. http://www.elperiodico.com.gt/es/20090117/pais/87032 and Bonillo, Cristina. "Norma Cruz y el derecho de la mujer; años de lucha por dignidad." *Prensa Libre.* 1 February 2009. http://www.prensalibre.com/pl/2009/febrero/01/290913.html

8. Reyes, Adrián. "Guatemala: Brutal Killings of Women Recall Counterinsurgency Techniques." *IPS News.* 22 June 2005. http://ipsnews.net/print.asp?idnews=29187

9. For more on the violence of Guatemala's armed conflict, see Sanford, Victoria. *Buried Secrets: Truth and Human Rights in Guatemala.* New York: Palgrave Macmillan, 2003.

10. Stop Violence Against Women. "Rape as a Tool of War: a Fact Sheet." Amnesty International USA. 2007. http://www.amnestyusa.org/women/rapeinwartime.html

11. See Guatemalan Commission for Historical Clarification (CEH). *Guatemala: Memory of Silence.* 1999. http://shr.aaas.org/guatemala/ceh/report/english/toc.html The systematic violence towards women has also been denounced in the United Nations Fourth World Conference on Women, Beijing Platform for Action. 1995. http://www.un.org/esa/gopher-data/conf/fwcw/off/a—20.en Made available by UN Department for Policy Coordination and Sustainable Development.

12. See CEH Report. In March of 1999, the Commission released its findings in *Guatemala: Memory of Silence,* reporting that 626 villages massacred, and approximately 1 million displaced. The CEH also found that the State was responsible for 93% of the arbitrary executions and 91% of the forced disappearances. Though to a lesser extent, guerrilla units also committed arbitrary executions and were responsible for 6% of the total violence.

13. CEH Report (Spanish), "La Violencia Sexual contra la Mujer," Chapter 2, Volume 3, #2. http://shr.aaas.org/guatemala/ceh/mds/spanish/cap2/vol3/mujer.html

14. Ibid., #38.

15. Ruhl, Katharine. "Guatemala's Femicides and the Ongoing Struggle for Women's Human Rights." Center for Gender and Refugee Studies, 21 (2006).

http://cgrs.uchastings.edu/documents/cgrs/cgrs_guatemala_femicides2.pdf In Huehuetenango's festival "Mujeres y guerra" the participants publicly recognized that sexual violence was not new to the civil war, but in reality an ongoing product of the unequal power relations between men and women. See "Declaración Política: Primer Festival regional por la memoria Mujeres y Guerra." News. *Nisgua: Working for Justice in Guatemala.* 27 November 2008. http://www.nisgua. org/news_analysis/index.asp?id=3275&mode=pf

16. CEH Report (Spanish), "La Violencia Sexual contra la Mujer," #41.

17. Human Rights Office of the Archdiocese of Guatemala. Guatemala. Never again! (Nunca Más). REHMI: Recovery of Historical Memory Project. The official report of the Human Rights Office, Archdiocese of Guatemala. Maryknoll: Orbis Books; 1999, Chapter 5, Case 7906. For more information on Bishop Juan Gerardi and his dedication to social justice and the REHMI project, see Goldman, Francisco. *The Art of Political Murder: Who Killed the Bishop?* New York: Grove Press, 2007.

18. Erturk, Yakin. "Integration of the Human Rights of Women and the Gender Perspective: Violence Against Women." Report of the Special Rapporteur on Violence Against Women, Its Causes and Consequences. Addendum: Mission to Guatemala. United Nations, Commission on Human Rights. Geneva: 10 February 2005. See also REHMI, Chapter 5, Interview 0803 and 0165, and CEH Report (Spanish), #74, 75.

19. Reyes, "Brutal Killings of Women."

20. REHMI, Chapter 5, *Botín de Guerra.* This disturbing trend is presently seen among gang members that target women in violent acts for different levels of "points." See "Guatemala: No Protection, No Justice: Killings of Women in Guatemala." Amnesty International. 2005. http://www.amnestyusa.org/document. php?lang=e&id=280F8FE94B2826C025

21. Ibid.

22. REHMI, Chapter 5, Case 1871.

23. Ibid. See also CEH Report (Spanish), #99.

24. Reyes, "Brutal Killings of Women."

29. See "Fracasa lucha contra maras." Nacional. *Prensa Libre.* 17 February 2009. http:// www.prensalibre.com/pl/2008/febrero/17/218992.html and "Guatemala: No Protection, No Justice." Amnesty International.

30. See "Guatemalan Police Rescue Kidnapped Woman, Arrest Two." *Latin American Herald Tribune.* 5 March 2009. http://www.laht.com/article. asp?CategoryId=23558&ArticleId=329115 and "Cops Could Be Behind Kidnappings in Guatemala." *Latin American Herald Tribune.* 9 March 2009. http:// www.laht.com/article.asp?CategoryId=23558&ArticleId=329337

31. See "Who Will Defend the Defenders: Criminalization of Human Rights Defenders and Chronic Impunity in Guatemala." Guatemala Human Rights Commission. December 2008. http://www.ghrc- usa.org/Programs/HumanRightsDefenders/ HumanRightsDefenders.htm

36. Orantes, "Cicig ve impunidad en casos de femicidio."

37. Ibid.

38. Guoz, Abner. "Onu: persiste impunidad y aumentan muertes violentas." Actualidad: Nacionales. *El Periódico.* 21 March 2007. http://www.elperiodico.com.gt/ es/20070321/actualidad/37938

39. Drysdale Walsh, Shannon. "Engendering Justice: Constructing Institutions to Address Violence Against Women." *Studies in Social Justice,* Vol. 2, No. 1 (2008), Page 7. http://ojs.uwindsor.ca/ojs/leddy/index.php/SSJ/article/view/668/578

40. Ibid.
41. For more information on the responsibilities of the Public Prosecutor's Office, see Ministerio Público. Preguntas Frecuentes. Ministerio Público de Guatemala, C.A. http://www.mp.gob.gt/preguntas_frecuentes.html
42. Ministerio Público. Organigrama Area de Fiscalía. Ministerio Público de Guatemala, C.A. http://www.mp.gob.gt/images/files/organigrama_area_fiscalia.pdf For additional information on the structure of Guatemala's Public Prosecutor's Office, see http://www.mp.gob.gt/organigramas.html
43. See *This World: Killer's Paradise*. Produced and Directed by Giselle Portenier. Reported by Olenka Frenkiel. Documentary. BBC Two, 2006. See also "Guatemala— Claudina Velásquez." Amnesty International USA. http://www.amnestyusa.org/individuals-at-risk/holiday-card-action/claudina- velasquez/page.do?id=1011294
44. See Sanford, "From Genocide to Femicide," and Amnesty International, "Guatemala: No Protection, No Justice."
45. Drysdale Walsh, 7.
46. See *This World: Killer's Paradise*. Most civilians choose to call the firefighters before the police, though there are hopes of change with a new police chief and greater accountability under President Colom's administration.
47. "PDH concluye estudio sobre femicidios." *La Hora, Suplemento Politico*. 14 April 2008. http://www.rel-uita.org/mujer/PDH-estudio_femicidios.htm
101. Juliani, Alida. "Guatemala Guerrilla Army of the Poor's Norma Cruz: Every Day We're Fighting to Save Lives." *Latin American Herald Tribune*. 18 January 2009. http://www.laht.com/article.asp?CategoryId=23558&ArticleId=325837
102. Update with Amanda Martin, GHRC Director, 27 February 2009.
103. Recommendation also from Baltazar Garzón, a magistrate of Spain's Criminal Court. "Impunidad se debe combatir sin que tiemble la mano, señala juez Garzón." Cerigua. 13 March 2009. http://cerigua.org/portal/index.php?option=com_content&task=view&id=8214&Itemid=1
104. GHRC, UDEFEGUA, GAM and CALDH recommendation. "Guatemalan Lawyer Gladys Monterroso Kidnapped and Tortured." Guatemala Human Rights Commission/USA. 25 March 2009. http://www.ghrcusa.org/Resources/UrgentActions/Gladys_urgentaction.htm
105. GHRC recommendation in Guatemala Policy Memo.
106. Fundación Sobrevivients. Conversation with Norma Cruz March 6, 2009.

In Israel Colonialization Brings Danger to Palestinian Women

Nadera Shalhoub-Kevorkian & Suhad Daher-Nashif

In the following excerpted viewpoint, Nadera Shalhoub-Kevorkian and Suhad Daher-Nashif describe how the killings of women and girls under the pretense of "honor" has become one of the greatest crises in Arab and Muslim societies. Specifically, this viewpoint focuses on the treatment of Palestinian women in the city of Ramleh, a city located within the country of Israel, and also posits how the information can be applied to cases of control and colonization as related to women in other countries. Shalhoub-Kevorkian is Chair in Law at the Hebrew University of Jerusalem. Daher-Nashif is a lecturer and researcher at Al-Qasimi College for Education.

As you read, consider the following questions:

1. Why is femicide one of the most pervasive human rights violations committed against Arab-Palestinian women and girls?
2. What has led to the Westernized misconception that "honor" killings are something intrinsic to Arab culture?
3. Per the viewpoint, how is the concept of colonization connected to violence against women?

"Femicide and Colonization : Between the Politics of Exclusion and the Culture of Control," by Nadera Shalhoub-Kevorkian and Suhad Daher-Nashif from *Violence Against Women* by Sage Publications, Inc. Reproduced with permission of Sage Publications, Inc. in the format Book via Copyright Clearance Center.

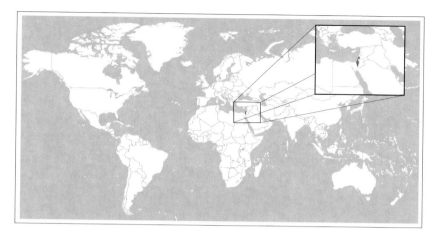

The murder of women and girls under the pretense of "honor" has emerged as one of the most sensationalized issues in the global media and feminist analyses alike, especially as they pertain to Arab and Muslim societies. Beyond the sensationalism, however, there is relatively little critical analysis exploring the social circumstances in which such murders take place, how they are positioned by and embedded in various systems, and the manners in which they are discursively constructed and represented.

The aim of this article is to analyze the ways in which the dialectic interrelationship between formal and informal legal-social systems constructs Palestinian women's murders within Israeli society, a relationship that functions in and is to a large extent empowered by a wider context of colonization. The main focus will be on the processes through which a national "politics of exclusion" colludes with a localized "culture of control" to generate the context within which violence against colonized women in colonial zones is fueled, strengthened, and even justified, by colonized and colonizer alike. The term politics of exclusion refers to the colonial mechanisms through which the Israeli state participates in the denial of the Palestinian people's rights to, among others, safety, housing, freedom of movement, political rights, economic development, education, and health. The term culture of control refers to localized manifestations of patriarchal and masculine logics that are empowered by the politics of exclusion.

The article is based on research conducted with the Palestinian community that lives within the borders of the State of Israel (and whose homeland was colonized in 1948). Specifically, the article focuses on the city of Ramleh, chosen due to both an increase in women being killed there over the past decade and its spatial significance. With most of its Palestinian residents expelled in 1948, Ramleh exists as a "contested" city with a Jewish majority and also a sizeable Palestinian minority. Like other "contested" cities in Israel, Ramleh is characterized by urban space designed to essentialize and segregate Arab-Palestinian and Jewish communities (see Yiftachel & Yacobi, 2003). In such "contested" cities, the Palestinian minority is subordinated spatially, socially, politically, and economically, producing an urban landscape that reproduces wider national interactions between "hegemonic oppression and minority reaction" (Yiftachel & Yacobi, 2003, p. 673). The case study of Ramleh is thus well positioned to explore the ways in which colonization constructs the daily lives of Palestinians in Israel, as well as to explore the complex social-legal and spatial effects of their exclusion by the Israeli state. In the context of the murder of Palestinian women, this specific case highlights the ways in which new forms of Empire have unleashed new tools of violence (Hardt & Negri, 2000; see also Abu-Lughod, 2002), and how these tools are used by members of local communities to justify violence against women.

Femicide, Representation, and the Politics of Naming

The term femicide is used in this article to refer to the murder of women and girls by a family member or members, whether this violence occurs within or outside of the confines of the home. In the Palestinian context, the concept of "femicide" was first used by Shalhoub-Kevorkian (2004) to denote "all violent acts that instill a perpetual fear in women or girls of being killed under the justification of 'honor'" (p. 10). Femicide remains one of the most pervasive human rights violations committed against Arab-Palestinian women and girls. It denies them safety and security, strips them of dignity, and undermines their ability to enjoy their fundamental right to life. The use of the term femicide is proposed to counter the common usage of the terms honor crimes or family honor crimes. Importantly, it signifies a refusal to accept the designation of the act of killing a woman or girl as "honorable" when perpetrated by a father, brother, or other family member. An argument is made for a broader categorization of such crimes, one that entails a clear rejection of the terminology of crimes of honor, or, as they are sometimes defined in Israel, "crimes committed on romantic basis" and in Western contexts "crimes of passion," as there is no honor, romance, or passion in such killings (Coomaraswamy, 2005).

Moreover, the use of the term femicide instead of honor killings is considered critical to counter dominant culturalized depictions of such crimes. Particularly in the context of Arab societies, discussions of femicide often draw on Orientalist depictions of "Arab culture," which are usually supported by shallow analyses that present Western societies as "cultureless" contrasted to those societies represented as the "Cultural Other" (Volpp, 2000). In this cultural framing, the killing of women for the purpose of family "honor" is simply something intrinsic to "Arab culture," which is purportedly violent, misogynistic, barbaric, and backward (Said, 1978). Although such culturalized explanations have never been sufficient or adequate when it comes to understanding femicide, they are especially important to challenge in this present period where imperial agendas deploy powerful images and icons of the oppression of Middle Eastern women as casus belli.

Avoiding engagement with the logics that drive sensationalized issues like femicide is clearly not a responsible approach for a Palestinian feminist. On one hand, it is contended that efforts to depoliticize acts of femicide by locating them entirely in the realm of "culture" are not only grossly misguided but also contribute to the construction of a racialized and racist framework that fails to address the murders of the Palestinian women effectively. Exploring the situation of Afghani women in the United States-led war on Afghanistan, Abu-Lughod (2002) argues that cultural logics prevent serious consideration of the roots and nature of human suffering (p. 784). Instead of seeking historical and political explanations, cultural framings encourage religiocultural ones rather than "questions that might lead to the exploration of global interconnections, we [are] offered ones that . . . artificially divide the world into separate spheres—recreating an imaginative geography of west versus east, us versus Muslims" (Abu-Lughod, 2002, p. 784). In the context of seriously addressing femicide among the Palestinian minority in Israel, it is imperative to avoid the simplistic and arguably imperializing connotations of the questions that arise out of the culturalized perspective.

On the other hand, it is critical to acknowledge that femicide—the killing of women by virtue of the fact that they are women—is a global epidemic. The limited Orientalist analysis of "dividing cultures into violent and violence free," as Shahrzad Mojab (2003) points out, "is in and of itself a patriarchal myth" (p. 2). Femicide exists in every country, cutting across boundaries of culture, class, education, income, ethnicity, and age. The global dimensions of this violence are alarming, as studies on its prevalence have highlighted (Coomaraswamy, 2005). No society can claim to be free of such violence, although there are of course variations in the patterns and trends of femicide within different regions, countries, and social groups (such as minorities, indigenous women, migrant women, refugee women, women living in the shadow of armed conflict, women with disabilities, female children, elderly women, and so on). The typical passivity toward tackling femicide displayed by the states worldwide and their law-enforcing machineries is evidence that it is neither a particular cultural phenomenon, nor is it one exclusive to Palestinians.

It is critical to address these cultural logics to the extent that they continue to frame discussions and policy outcomes on issues of gender-based violence (GBV), particularly in Arab and Muslim communities. In this vein, this article attempts to set forth a framework of analysis that moves beyond essentializing cultural logics to show how economic, political, and social processes create spaces for articulations of "Palestinian culture"—as if it were a static context—that justifies the crime of femicide. Such articulations, in turn, are appropriated, selectively deployed, and circulated in global discourses and analyses of GBV that continue to project femicide as a "crime of honor," rather than a crime that is fueled by the interplay between a colonial politics of exclusion and a localized culture of control.

[…]

Colonization, and the Interrelationship Between Formal and Informal Systems

Subject to Israeli control, Palestinian society is in a state of continuous colonization, spurred by a process of national Judaization (Yiftachel, 1998; Zureik, 1979). As much as this colonization is clearly rendered differently for Palestinians inside Israel than it is for those "outside" of it in the West Bank and the Gaza Strip, it is important to acknowledge the centrality of colonialism to Palestinian understandings and experiences. While the fields of colonial and postcolonial studies provide numerous definitions of the term colonialism, in its broadest sense it refers to the subjugation of one people by another. Colonialism is thus a relation of unequal power, that is, a form of domination and (political) control of a territory and population by a state (Horvarth, 1972). The coercion exercised by the colonizer is typically justified by some kind of ideology that regularly implies the perception of the superiority of the colonizer over the colonized population (see Fanon, 1968; Said, 1978). Colonialism is often further understood to imply some form of economic exploitation (Horvarth, 1972), as well as a "process of culture-change" of the colonized people, in which the colonizer attempts to impose a new—his—cultural order on the colonized population (Merry, 1991, p. 894). In the case of Palestinians inside Israel, all these facets of colonialism collude to produce a complicated set of circumstances, circumstances explored here through the prism of femicide.

This article comprehends the colonial situation in which the Palestinian community in Israel lives through Agamben's (2005) notion of "state of exception." "States of exception" are the spaces where the laws of sovereign states—such as those prohibiting killing or concerned with promoting accepted standards of justice—no longer apply, and it is, as Carl Schmitt asserts, the sovereign power (in this case, Israel) who decides upon the state of exception (cited in Agamben, 2005, p. 1). This state of exception forges a situation in which Palestinian society is simultaneously excluded and included; excluded as "security" and "demographic" threats to the Jewish state, but included by virtue of Israel's political control over Palestinian lives and the spaces in which they live them. It is a state in which life is "bare," and in which death, too, is bare, particularly in the case of women. With the social constructed by the political (and vice versa), the political condition in which Palestinians find themselves participates in the construction of Palestinian social structures. It is hence the colonial condition that plays a role in constructing issues of the status of women and gender relations within Palestinian society. Projects of colonization aim, in part, at excluding the Other, and colonization scripts relations of domination over the land as well as the bodies of people. Women's bodies, sexuality, and spaces are one of the means through which such projects proceed.

This wider colonial context both frames and generates a complex interrelationship between informal Palestinian systems and the formal Israeli legal system, resulting in the Palestinian community living what could be conceptualized as a hybrid and liminal state of existence (Yiftachel & Yacobi, 2003). These informal structures, which include systems of kinship, patriarchy, and the traditional tribal system, continue to play a role in defining the physical and social boundaries within which female and male individuals are able to move and act. They are primary contributors to the regulation of social behavior, roles, responsibilities, and relations among members of Palestinian society in general. Such regulation is achieved through the enforcement of social norms and codes of "honor" that define and delimit, among others, one's mobility, choice of spouse, type and level of education, dress, profession, and sexual behavior. Holding onto the concept of "honor" serves the purpose of preserving the social power of informal structures and fulfilling their material and social interests.

Israel's ongoing control over the Palestinian minority has in many ways empowered and strengthened these informal structures, with many Palestinians rejecting Israeli formal systems and institutes as forms of collaboration with or extensions of the colonizer. This is particularly true in the context of informal structures that pertain to questions of "honor" and the regulation of women's bodies and lives, something too which can be understood as a reaction to Israeli systems of control over the Palestinian minority. As Foucault (1980) states, one reaction to control exercised by an external power is to return this control to the external power itself, which can be done in several ways. In the Palestinian context, the imbalance of external Israeli and internal Palestinian control (Israelis hold and control the power, while Palestinians wield far less power and are controlled) means that "returning control" tends to be more directed at community insiders who have less power—primarily women, but also children, the handicapped and the elderly. Exercising control over women, especially their sexuality, constitutes a patriarchal means of maintaining control of and managing the internal social equilibrium.

Power, as Foucault (1980) reminds us, is productive, in the sense that it produces types of behaviors and events. Israeli power and control produces types of social behavior, including behavior that empowers informal systems and control over marginal groups within Palestinian society. Women's bodies become sites of struggle for internal control, and femicide is a form of self-destruction that results from external control exercised by colonial powers (see Fanon, 1963, for a deeper explanation of such dynamics).

[...]

Findings

The number of Palestinian women citizens of Israel killed in confirmed femicide cases over the past decade numbers approximately 76. Of these, five were killed in 2000, nine in 2001, one in 2002, four in 2003, five in 2004, eight in 2005, nine in 2006,ten in 2007, six in 2008, nine in 2009, ten in 2010, nine in 2011 and five in 2012. Comparatively a relatively high rate of femicide cases took place between the years of 2000 and 2007 in the Al-Gawareesh neighborhood of Ramleh, the focus of our case study; indeed, more cases were confirmed here than in any other Palestinian town inside Israel. Most of the victims were killed by their brothers and other male relatives, often cousins. Given that Al-Gawareesh is spatially, economically and socially excluded from wider Ramleh, a complex picture emerged from the research, in which social, religious, political, legal and spatial processes combine to construct the crime of femicide.

Not a long time ago they came and told me that my turn was next. They have a list, every woman knows if she's on this list or not. If you are on the list, it doesn't matter whether you did something or not, they will find a reason to say you behaved badly. If a woman has a cellular phone, they might kill her. If she talked with someone they might kill her. We have men in the family who hate women. . . . It's enough for someone to say something about a girl or a woman, that's it. One guy might provoke and anger the entire family, turning them against the woman. Afterward they will begin the planning, what they will do with her. Sometimes they work on the plan for a whole year, and the whole time she is aware of the fact that they plan to kill her, until they kill her. If the woman knows that there is a plan to kill her, sometimes she goes to the heads and elders of the family to ask them do something to calm the situation. But they can't help all the time. The problem is that when they construct their murder plan they fear no one. After they complete their plan, they decide who will do it.

In El Salvador Women Are Not Protected Against Violence

Angelika Albaladejo

In the following viewpoint, Angelika Albaladejo describes the specific cases of violence faced by the women who live in El Salvador. While men are equally as likely to be murdered as women in this country, nearly a quarter of women in El Salvador have been the victim of sexual violence. Not only that, but due to a lack of trust in the judicial system, women often do not report the violence that they face, and are even harassed when they attempt to protect their male family members from gang-related persecution. Albaladejo is an independent multimedia journalist who covers security and rights in the Americas.

As you read, consider the following questions:

1. Per the viewpoint, how many Salvadoran women have suffered some form of violence in their lives?
2. Why do Salvadoran women face little protection from rape and other forms of feminine-centered violence?
3. What are the reasons why women in El Salvador do not report violence? What can be done to help these women?

The violence gripping El Salvador affects women in a different way than men. Within the current security crisis, gang and

"How Violence Affects Women in El Salvador," by Angelika Albaladejo, Latin America Working Group Education Fund, February 22, 2016. Reprinted with permission from Latin America Working Group Education Fund, www.lawg.org.

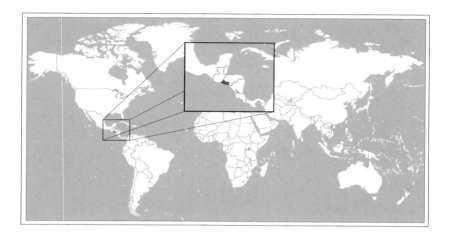

security force violence has exacerbated a broader, long-standing acceptance of violence against women. More than half of all Salvadoran women say they have suffered some form of violence in their lives. Over a quarter of these women were victims of sexual or physical violence.

While men are far more likely to be murdered, women are significantly more likely to experience intrafamilial, sexual, or economic violence. To make matters worse, women receive little to no guarantees of protection from the state. Due to ineffective governmental institutions, corruption, and social acceptance, impunity reigns in nearly all cases of violence against women.

At work, many women face discrimination and abuse ranging from wage and pension theft by business owners to extortion by gangs. More than half of all working Salvadoran women are employed in the informal sector, placing them at higher risk of exploitation and extortion because the state does not regulate these jobs.

Women often face the highest levels of violence in their own homes. In the first nine months of 2015, the Attorney General's Special Attention Unit for Women attended to 1,283 cases of intrafamilial violence against women. While this represents an average of almost five reports each day, the true number is almost certainly higher as many cases of domestic violence go unreported.

The prevalence of sexual violence against women in El Salvador is also staggering. Between January and August 2015, the National Civilian Police (PNC) registered an average of nearly five cases per day of sexual violence against women, including rape and sexual assault. And victims are often the most vulnerable—more than half of these assaults were carried out against girls, adolescents, and the disabled.

On top of the everyday violence already faced by women, ongoing gang conflict has led to an increase in some of the most heinous acts of violence against women. In the past, sexual violence was primarily committed in the home by a family member. Now however, rape and sexual assault are increasingly committed by gangs and security forces.

Gangs rape and violently murder young girls, or claim them as "novias de las pandillas" – "girlfriends" of the gangs. "Women's bodies were treated like territory during the civil war and continue to be today by the gangs," says Jeanette Urquilla, the director of the Organization of Salvadoran Women for Peace (ORMUSA). In many gang-controlled neighborhoods, young girls expect they will be raped, abducted, and/or murdered by the gangs. Urquilla says this has led some families to pressure young women to become pregnant with their boyfriends, rather than be claimed by a gang member.

Police officers and soldiers stationed in "barrios calientes"—high-violence or gang-controlled neighborhoods—have also been linked to cases of sexual violence. In one case, a 13-year-old girl with Down syndrome was raped by soldiers stationed in her community, according to eyewitness reports from members of a human rights group. In another case, a soldier was arrested in February 2016 on charges of abducting, raping, and threatening the life of a young woman.

As "mano dura" or heavy-handed policing expands in El Salvador, the targeting of teenage boys suspected of gang affiliation is also having an inadvertent impact on women. Female family members who attempt to protect their male relatives from arrest or harassment are being threatened and attacked themselves. In a recently released documentary, a VICE News camera crew captured a raid on the home of a suspected gang member where the women and children were visibly intimidated by the presence of heavily armed security forces entering in the middle of the night.

The targeted killing of women based on their gender, known as femicide, is also on the rise. An estimated 2,521 women have been murdered in El Salvador since 2009; this represents an average of 420 femicides each year. And according to the Observatory of Violence Against Women, the numbers are escalating. In the first ten months of 2015, 475 women were murdered—an average of one femicide every 16 hours.

For many reasons, women often don't report violence. Vanda Pignato, El Salvador's Secretary of Social Inclusion, told La Prensa Gráfica that women stay silent because of "fear, shame, terror, and above all, because they do not trust the judicial system. The judicial system in El Salvador leaves much to be desired on this issue. There is widespread impunity for aggressors and that isn't a good message for young people and the female victims of violence."

Even officials within government institutions sometimes commit violence against those they are charged to protect. Patterns of impunity validate this "masculinity" within the institutions, which leads to further violence, says a program coordinator for ORMUSA. In 12 percent of the cases of violence against women reported to ORMUSA, the alleged perpetrators were judges, prosecutors, lawyers, and police officers. In one case, a woman brought charges against her husband, a PNC officer, for firing his weapon and injuring her. The victim later withdrew her testimony, clearing the officer, even though neighbors and other police officers on the scene heard the attack and witnessed her husband dragging her across the floor.

The Salvadoran government has begun to implement some programs and legislation to combat violence against women. But progress has been slow, in part because the violence is perceived as a social problem outside of the government's realm of responsibility. Nevertheless, some important mechanisms for addressing violence against women have been created in recent years due to the efforts of Salvadoran feminist organizations. In 2010, the Salvadoran legislature passed a set of framework laws—constitutional provisions that lay out general obligations for governmental institutions— known as the "Comprehensive Special Law for a Life without Violence for Women." Civil society groups drafted this legislation to address violence against women through "prevention, special attention, prosecution and punishment." However, to date, less than half of all Salvadoran institutions have worked to implement the law.

Some of these obligations were codified into law in 2011 with the passage of legislation that requires the Attorney General's office to create "Special Protection Units" focused on intrafamilial violence, gender-based violence, and discrimination against women. These units are supposed to offer legal representation, accept and investigate reports, provide psychological and social attention during the case, and develop a system for referring cases to government institutions and local gender units. The Attorney General's office also established "Self-Help Groups" to give direct assistance to victims within their local community. These groups provide women with a space to discuss intrafamilial violence and seek help with their cases. Impact studies indicate that these groups have been successful in empowering women to leave abusive relationships.

To date, the police have rolled out eleven local "Gender Units" to provide attention to female victims of violence. These special police units are trained with a gender-focused curriculum and collaborate with local women to create "fear maps" pinpointing high-risk areas and the types of violence specific to the community. The Gender Units are meant to use the fear maps to take targeted actions like increasing officer patrols on a dimly lit street where rapes have taken place. While these special police units have had some success, the constant rotation of personnel makes it difficult for officers to build relationships with the local community. Many women don't even know these units exist due to limited outreach and a lack of public awareness campaigns.

Although these laws and specialized units represent positive steps forward by the Salvadoran government, they haven't been fully implemented and access to these programs is very limited. These frameworks also fail to address widespread impunity and do not provide adequate protection for those reporting crimes. Long-standing institutional barriers continue to block access to programs for reporting and escaping violence. For example, there is little to no access to shelters or relocation centers for female victims of violence. The Salvadoran Institute for the Development of Women (ISDEMU) provides temporary assistance for women fleeing domestic abuse, but it is unable to accept entire families, which discourages many victims from seeking help. In addition, the Inter-American Commission on Human Rights found that Supreme Court centers for reporting domestic or intrafamilial violence are ineffective, inaccessible, and discriminatory.

The United States has invested in "multi-institutional assistance centers" for victims of gender-based violence (GBV), which USAID asserts have "supported efforts to reduce levels of impunity and promote fairness in treatment of GBV survivors." A sample study of one center showed that of the 99 domestic violence cases received, "all were presented in court and 97 of them resulted in convictions." While these isolated cases do not reflect an overall change in the levels of impunity in violent crimes against women, it is possible that such models might merit further investigation.

In addition to insecurity and impunity, the country's healthcare system has placed women at further risk by striping them of legal control over their reproductive health. El Salvador has maintained some of the most draconian abortion laws in the world for over two decades, criminalizing abortion even in cases of rape or when the pregnancy poses a risk to the mother's life.

Since abortion and miscarriage were criminalized in 1998, 129 women have been prosecuted for "homicide," including women imprisoned for having a miscarriage or a stillbirth.

The Citizens' Association for the Decriminalization of Abortion, a prominent organization advocating for changes to El Salvador's abortion laws, estimates that over 35,000 insecure clandestine abortions have taken place in El Salvador since 1998.

Women's mental health is also negatively affected by the country's approach to reproductive healthcare paired with mounting levels of violence. "There's a correlation between sexual violence and the high rate of suicides among adolescents—that's the reality," a Salvadoran health official told Reuters. "Pregnancy is a determining factor behind teenage suicides."

Suicide is now the third most common cause of death for pregnant women overall and accounts for 57 percent of the deaths of pregnant girls between the ages of 10 and 19.

In spite of national and international pressure on the Salvadoran government to revoke these damaging laws and release the unjustly imprisoned women, the Ministry of Health has blocked advances in women's healthcare. Urquilla says the ministry fears political backlash from religious and conservative groups, as well as the legislature. These conservative views, while strongest in the ARENA party, stretch across party lines and are shared by some FMLN politicians.

However, El Salvador's strict anti-abortion laws have been further called into question with the recent and rapid spread of the mosquito-borne Zika virus thought to be linked to birth defects. The Salvadoran health minister has said that from a public health perspective, the total criminalization of abortion is a "true difficulty" that may place women and their babies at risk. However, the Salvadoran legislature has not taken action to change the laws.

The Salvadoran government, in line with several other Latin American countries, has advised women not to get pregnant until 2018, placing the burden of responsibility on women who often have little control over their own bodies due to high rates of sexual violence, repressive laws, and a lack of access to reproductive healthcare.

As security conditions in El Salvador worsen, violence against women continues to increase in severity. To address these issues, the Salvadoran government will need to implement existing legislation, expand institutional capacity, increase protection for victims of violence, and perhaps most importantly, work with Salvadoran civil society groups to begin to shift the cultural, social, and economic dynamics currently reinforcing impunity and acceptance of violence against women.

In South Africa Women Are Not Granted Control of Their Health

Pieter Fourie

In the following viewpoint, an excerpt from a study about the context of sexual-based politics as related to South Africa's HIV/ AIDS epidemic, Pieter Fourie details how the government impacts women's ability to make decisions about their health. Additionally, Fourie concludes that policy makers in the South African government must do more to create gender-specific policies that can transform public service and minimize the number of deaths, even on a daily basis, faced by those impacted by HIV/AIDS. Fourie is a pediatrician, engineer, and adjunct professor at Stellenbosch University in Cape Town, South Africa.

As you read, consider the following questions:

1. What can be done to stabilize the impact of HIV/AIDS in South Africa?
2. Per the viewpoint, how is the HIV/AIDS epidemic in South Africa connected to feminism?
3. How does sexual violence relate to the spread of HIV/ AIDS in South Africa?

"Liberal Feminism and HIV/AIDS in South Africa: Hindrance or Help in Decision Making?" by Pieter Fourie, International Political Science Association. Reprinted by permission of Pieter Fourie, Stellenbosch University.

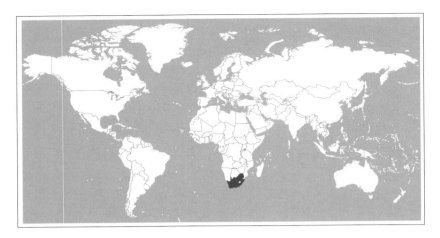

South Africans are dying of AIDS at a rate of around 1,000 people every day. That is the equivalent of more than one 9/11 attack on South Africans every three days, 365 days a year—and this number is steadily increasing. Since AIDS first officially made its appearance in this country in 1982, South Africa's policy response to HIV and AIDS has been ineffectual, despite the formulation and ostensible introduction of several public policy HIV and AIDS interventions by consecutive governments. Analysts are in agreement that national infection rates will only stabilise after 2006—this will not be on account of effective policies, however, but rather as a consequence of the natural saturation point of the epidemic.

However, stabilisation does not mean that the impact of HIV and AIDS in South Africa will decrease: at the household level families will have to cope with the ongoing tragedy of losing loved ones, whilst the economy will continue to suffer under the impact of the epidemic. In 2006 alone HIV and AIDS are expected to infect more than 500,000 people in South Africa, and since these people are—in the absence of ARVs—sure to die over the next few years, the imperative to implement an appropriate and effective public programmatic response is clear.

AIDS Statistics for South Africa (2006)

AIDS deaths per day	947
New HIV infections per day	1,443
People living with HIV	5,372,476
Total AIDS deaths	345,640
Total new HIV infections	526,771
Total AIDS sick	576,963
Adults with AIDS, not on ARVs	502,468
Children with AIDS, not on ARVs	26,883
Adults on ARVs	154,832
Children on ARVs	20,050

SOURCE: Nicolay (2006:2)

Social theory has been surprisingly quiet on the social determinants of HIV in South Africa. One could speculate on the causes for this—maybe the sexual nature of the subject made it anathema in a morally conservative society; possibly the issue remains so racialised and politicised in this country that social theorists elect to focus on other issues instead. Whatever the case may be, this intellectual silence can only contribute to entrenching existing culture, belief systems and, in the end, patriarchy, which compounds the societal determinants that make the gendered impact of AIDS even worse.

This paper will, in the first instance, consider some of the manifestations of HIV and AIDS as a gendered variable. This will be followed by a brief review of the basic feminist theories— what the lessons are that these afford us when combined with the societal effects of the epidemic. This is done within the context of contemporary South Africa as a state with a liberal constitution. It would not be incorrect to take as our point of departure that the feminism tolerated by patriarchy in South Africa is the liberal feminist variant—focusing more on state institutions and liberal legislation, and less on the biological, social and class/race foci of other feminist strains. Noting the failure of this liberal "national gender machinery," the paper interrogates manners in which South Africa's existing national AIDS policy can be gender mainstreamed.

[…]

HIV and AIDS as a Gendered Variable

Physiology

Women are physiologically at a greater risk than men of contracting HIV through heterosexual modes of transmission. O'Sullivan (2000:26) notes that

- [i]n Africa the number of women infected with HIV outnumbers infected men. Twelve point two million African women are living with HIV/AIDS as compared to 10.1 million men...young African women between the ages of 15 and 19 are four to six times more likely to be HIV-positive than young men of the same ages. Women are more easily infected with HIV when they have sex with a positive man than when a man has sex with a positive woman.... Women's economic, social, sexual and cultural subordination and inequality make frighteningly material impacts on each positive women's life.

- Mboi (1996:97-98) tells us that the shape of the vagina, larger mucosal area of women, and greater viral inoculum present in semen compared with vaginal secretions are all suggested as key factors. Not only do familial relations facilitate the spread of the disease amongst the female population; stereotypical gender roles place women at greater risk of contracting it from their sexual partners.

Rape

South African women have a one in four chance of being subjected to gender-based violence. Rape is an act of sexual aggression. It is used as a weapon or tool of aggression by men against women. What makes it so applicable within the African context is the effect that rape has on the social or human security of communities in war-torn areas. Rape and the use of it as a vector for the pro-active spread of HIV/AIDS has become a symptom of societal sickness. This and other forms of sexual violence—such as forced prostitution—are frequently used in war (e.g. in the Balkans and more recently in Sierra Leone) for a number of reasons. "Rape is an outlet for the sexual aggression of combatants and it is related to the idea that women are war booty; it is used to spread terror and loss of morale; and it is used to undermine women's ability to sustain their communities during times of conflict" (Matthews, 2000:18). Lately, there have been reports of the "corrective rape" of (particularly black) lesbians in South African society—rape thus used as a tool to violently heterosexualise so-called gender deviancy out of these women.

Compounding this, Shell (2000:19) mentions the birth of a diabolical new profile of rapists in South Africa: "Township residents ... term such people 'Jack Rollers' which another national authority defined in a glossary as 'Township youth who purposefully infect young women with HIV by raping them. This is a relatively new phenomenon in South Africa and the youth who do this are said to be unemployed and frustrated young men who have found out that they are HIV positive and say that they want to die with others.'" Another dangerous myth that perpetuates rape is the belief that sexual intercourse with a female virgin will cure AIDS (Shell & Zeitlin, 2000:8). The result, of course, is that HIV is spread violently to this sector of the female community.

The practical effect is that the epidemic is likely to cause crime in more direct ways. The belief that sex with a virgin can cure HIV and AIDS appears to be wide-spread in Southern Africa (Leclerc-Madlala, 1996:35), with 25 per cent of young South Africans not knowing that this is a myth (LoveLife, 2000). Moreover, rapists may also be targeting young girls in the belief that being less sexually active, they are also less likely to have HIV or AIDS (Leclerc-Madlala, 1996:35-36). A study conducted among urban South African township youth in 1996 found that for young people the knowledge that they were infected with HIV or merely believed that they might be infected "was accepted not only as a death sentence but also as a passport to sexual licence" (Leclerc-Madlala, 1996:32). That is, some youths argue that they would actively spread HIV among as many people as possible if they themselves were infected with HIV—a philosophy of "infect one, infect all." Young women expressed a general fear that men would respond to an HIV-positive diagnosis by raping women (Leclerc-Madlala, 1996:33-34).

A study of Tanzanian women found an association between physical violence and HIV-infection. HIV-positive women were more likely to have had a physically violent partner in their lifetime. HIV-positive women under 30 were ten times more likely to report violence than non-infected women of the same age group (Maman et al, 2001). "The strong, consistently positive relationship between a prior history of violence and HIV-infection lends support to the theory that violence may play a role in women's risk for HIV-infection" (Vetten & Bhana, 2001:12).

Gender Roles & Culture

Women are culturally disempowered to negotiate sexual intercourse with their male partners—if the latter insist on so-called dry sex (which greatly compounds women's susceptibility to HIV), women have very little say in the matter. Also, women are socially subordinate—they have very little if any say in whether protection can or should be used during intercourse (O'Sullivan, 2000:29), access to female condoms is limited (Monekosso, 1997:6), and medical research institutions do not put any great priority on the development of "stealth" protective measures aimed at the female market such as sperm-and microbicides (Gottemoeller, 2000). Stereotypical gender roles thus place women at greater risk to HIV/AIDS in Southern Africa.

Another contributing factor is the fact that young girls are often married off to much older men. This compounds these women's silence: they are materially and socially dependent on men and simply do not have the social and economic resources to claim control over their own vulnerability to the disease. As Ndiaye (2000:61) points out:

> Early marriages place African women in a vulnerable position, as they are passively exposed to risks incurred by having many sexual partners through the behaviour of their husbands. For a man in many African cultures, it is a sign of virility to have multiple sexual partners. Thus, women are often infected by their polygamous husbands or by their partners who adopt risky sexual practices—sex with a number of women, or prostitutes, or with other men.

It has also become acceptable—quite explicitly in Zulu culture with support from the Zulu King himself—to engage in "virginity testing" of young women and girls. This of course not only violates these women, but places an onus of culpability for AIDS on anyone who is young and female. For the most part, the men are absent (Siplon, 2005).

Compounding these factors, in many instances African customary law entrenches women's economic insecurity. In Zambia, for instance, widows of AIDS casualties are often victim to instances of "property-grabbing"—the law allowing or not acting against in- laws who claim the land of the diseased family member (Kinghorn, 1994). Also, society's dependence on women and girls as care-givers within the household makes it impossible or very difficult for females to enter the public sphere and realm of political decision-making. In a sense, then, these traditional conceptions of mothering means that the "private" is not allowed to become "public," and the result is that women remain impotent, suppressed, and thus societally and economically excluded. As Mboi (1996:97) emphasises,

> Gender expectations/roles are crucial in determining if or how a woman may protect herself, her sexual partner(s), even her unborn child from HIV infection. Within [developing countries] widely held stereotypes about what is "proper" and "normal" for men and women regarding sexual feeling and expression

AIDS on the Decline

Today is World AIDS Day, and three neighboring countries in southern Africa that have been hard-hit by HIV received remarkably good news.

As part of a massive, first-of-its-kind survey, researchers randomly visited households in Malawi, Zambia, and Zimbabwe and tested about 80,000 people for HIV. In each country, more than 86% of the people receiving antiretroviral treatment had fully suppressed HIV, which means viral levels are so low they are not detectable on standard blood tests. This not only staves off AIDS, but makes it highly unlikely that they will infect others. The rate of new infections has also plummeted by more than 50% in the region since 2003. "We were amazed when we saw this," says Wafaa El-Sadr, an epidemiologist who heads an international health-strengthening program called ICAP at Columbia University Mailman School of Public Health, which led the survey. "It's really a credit to these countries—and they're not the world's richest places."

The three countries since 2004 collectively have received nearly $4 billion from the U.S. President's Emergency Plan for AIDS Relief (PEPFAR), which gave ICAP $125 million to conduct what are known as population-based HIV impact assessments (PHIAs) in 12 sub-Saharan African countries and Haiti. The aim is to help the countries and PEPFAR better target prevention and treatment efforts. The preliminary findings announced today are the first data reported from these assessments. "It's pretty doggone amazing," says Deborah Birx, who heads PEPFAR in Washington, D.C. "This really shows us why it's so important to get community level survey data."

Until now, the most authoritative estimates of HIV infection rates, or incidence, and prevalence have come from the Joint United Nations Programme on HIV/AIDS (UNAIDS) in Geneva, Switzerland. Those are based on mathematical models that largely extrapolate from clinics and nonrandomized surveys conducted by countries. The more rigorous PHIA approach "largely confirms" the UNAIDS estimates, says epidemiologist Peter Ghys, who directs strategic information and evaluation there. The most notable exception is PHIA found an incidence of 0.45 in Zimbabwe in 2016, which is almost half the 0.88 reported by UNAIDS in 2015. (The PHIA assessed adults between 15 and 64 years of age, whereas UNAIDS estimates are for 15- to 49-year-olds.)

"Southern Africa's AIDS Epidemic Takes Nosedive," by Jon Cohen, American Association for the Advancement of Science, December 1, 2016.

severely limit the latitude most women have (or will exercise) for action in the micro-settings where sexual divisions are made. In general "knowledge," "pleasure," "rights" and "initiative" belong to men, while "innocence," "acceptance" and "duty" are portrayed as "normal" for women.

HIV and AIDS and Feminist Ideologies

From the preceding section it is clear that the different socio-cultural and biological manifestations of HIV/AIDS expose how a gender-sensitive analytical lens could contribute to greater insight into (and counteraction of) the virus's impact in African society. In an ideal world, where public policies are actually responsive to social exigencies, insights afforded by such a normative, gender lens could potentially facilitate societal transformation.

Having said that, one should question whether our liberal constitution is enough to transform society and achieve such a wish list. Can liberal feminism alone counter the socio-economic impact of a patriarchy that finds application beyond legislation and state institutions? Any ideology is a double-edged sword: it describes reality as much as it prescribes an ideal, and this paper argues that liberal feminism comes up short on both scores.

The examples of HIV and AIDS as a gendered variable cited above were chosen with more in mind than for their mere illustrative value. Female physiological risk demonstrates the reality of women's biological vulnerability, compounded by the horrible scale of rape in this country. Homophobia, on the other hand, demonstrates the socio-cultural bias that is constructed and passed on from one generation to the next, and applied to stigmatise some HIV-positive individuals in the process. Also, sexual myths such as virgin sex as a cure for HIV (and other practices) expose how society constructs spurious social vaccines as a way of coping with the impact of the epidemic.

What can social theory—particularly the variety of feminist ideologies—teach us to debunk such myths, creating a society more fully able to effectively respond to the reality of HIV/AIDS?

One premise of radical feminism is that women are subjugated by a patriarchal control of biomedical sphere. Women are excluded and suppressed due to their biological "otherness"; their "unmaleness." Can we not benefit from radical feminism's emphasis on the impact of biology on women's oppression—for does HIV not affect women physiologically much more aggressively and make women more vulnerable and susceptible to disease?

In addition, is it not a gross theoretical oversight to discount Marxist feminism's insistence that we examine the class divisions entrenched by a disease that places most of the burden of care (for the sick, the very young, the aged) on the female members of society, and the "girl child" specifically? This is particularly true for South Africa, where the sexual division of labour and its concomitant class implications have been politicised and racialised as much as they have been gendered. After all, who is left to work the land, look after the sick, the old, the very young once the economically active sections of society have been wiped out? Marxist feminism tells us that such an insidious burden of care removes women from the public domain and—at the very basic level—nefariously impacts on young women's ability to ever enter the public domain and achieve even the most basic political empowerment.

And lastly, could we not benefit enormously by taking into account what socialist feminism teaches us about individuals as social constructs—not only in the public domain, but also in the private domain? This goes to the core of our socio-cultural ways of operating as gendered individuals within society as much as within the family. Socialist feminism par excellence reveals the social constructive impact of our cultures and the compounding impact that has on the societal effects of HIV and AIDS. To cite the examples noted in this paper, this variant of feminism exposes homophobia, mythologies around HIV/AIDS and rape as a social constructs.

Periodical and Internet Sources Bibliography

The following articles have been selected to supplement the diverse views presented in this chapter.

Kara Alaimo "Women Should Be Vanguard of the Gun-Control Movement," Bloomberg, May 30, 2018. https://www.bloomberg.com/view/articles/2018-05-30/women-should-be-leading-the-fight-for-stricter-gun-laws

Steve Bullock, "On Guns, We're as Paralyzed as I Was the Day My Nephew Was Shot: Montana Governor," *USA Today*, May 30, 2018. https://www.usatoday.com/story/opinion/2018/05/30/america-wants-action-gun-violence-end-paralysis-column/651241002/

Catholic News Service, "So-called Honor Killing in Catholic Family Shocks Indian State," *National Catholic Reporter,* May 30, 2018. https://www.ncronline.org/news/world/so-called-honor-killing-catholic-family-shocks-indian-state

Nina Feldman, "After Years of Domestic Violence, a Gun Changed Everything," *Philadelphia Tribune,* June 1, 2018. http://www.phillytrib.com/news/after-years-of-domestic-violence-a-gun-changed-everything/article_b1a66ea7-87bb-5aa5-92ac-271ba42e6767.html

Karen Fratti, "6 Things You Can Do Right Now to Help Stop Gun Violence That Aren't "Thoughts and Prayers," Hello Giggles, June 1, 2018. https://hellogiggles.com/news/how-to-stop-gun-violence/

Stephanie Höppner, "'Honor Killings' in Germany: When Families Turn Executioners," DW.com, February 8, 2018. http://www.dw.com/en/honor-killings-in-germany-when-families-turn-executioners/a-42511928

Saroop Ijaz, "'Honor' Killings Continue in Pakistan Despite New Law," Human Rights Watch, September 25, 2017. https://www.hrw.org/news/2017/09/25/honor-killings-continue-pakistan-despite-new-law

Christina Maza, "Honor Killings, Rape, Acid Attacks and Child Abuse Rampant in Pakistan, Reports Claim," Newsweek, March 13, 2018. http://www.newsweek.com/honor-killings-rape-acid-attacks-and-child-abuse-rampant-pakistan-reports-842324

Chris Mueller, "Fox Cities Residents Speak Out Against Gun Violence," *Post Crescent,* June 1, 2018. https://www.postcrescent.com/story/news/2018/06/01/fox-cities-residents-speak-out-against-gun-violence/663594002/

Sune Engel Rasmussen, "'Honour' Killings in Karachi Shock Pakistan's Largest City," *Guardian,* December 27, 2017. https://www.theguardian.com/world/2017/dec/27/honour-killings-in-karachi-shock-pakistans-largest-city

Reuters, "Pakistan Police Arrest Two in Suspected 'Honor Killing' of Italian Woman," Business Insider, May 10, 2018. http://www.businessinsider.com/r-pakistan-police-arrest-two-in-suspected-honor-killing-of-italian-woman-2018-5

Frances Wilson, "School Shootings Are Like Domestic Violence, Amplified," *Caller Times,* May 31, 2018. https://www.caller.com/story/opinion/2018/05/31/school-shootings-like-domestic-violence-amplified/661219002/

GLOBALVIEWPOINTS

CHAPTER 3

Religion and Violence Against Women

In Turkey a Change in Consciousness Is Needed to Stop Honor Killings

Zulfu Livaneli

In the following viewpoint, Zulfu Livaneli discusses the report from the Turkish National Assembly regarding violence against women and children, specifically regarding "honor" crimes. Along with breaking down the most common reasons for honor-based violence in Turkey, Livaneli details how this type of violence has been spreading throughout the entirety of the European Union. While legal measures have been passed in many countries, including Turkey, Livaneli posits that law alone will not be enough to solve the problem of violence against women in that country. Livaneli is a Turkish musician, author, poet, and politician.

As you read, consider the following questions:

1. What are the two most common forms of honor-based violence in Turkey?
2. Per the viewpoint, how many women are victim of "honor killings" each year? Is this number accurate? Why or why not?
3. What steps have been taken by the EU to curb violence against women in Europe? Have these changes been effective? Why or why not?

"Honor Killings and Violence Against Women in Turkey," by Zulfu Livaneli, Turkish Culture Portal, http://www.turkishculture.org/lifestyles/turkish-culture-portal/the-women/honor-killings-426.htm?type=1. This article is brought to you for free and open access by Turkish Culture.

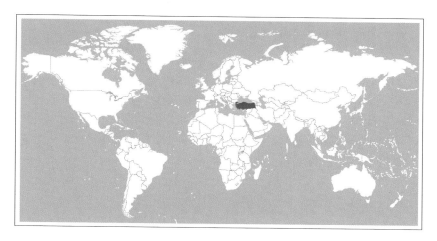

The Turkish National Assembly has recently published an extensive report on violence against women and children in general and the case of honor crimes in particular. This report is important in that it includes the first official statistical data regarding honor crimes. According to the report, 1091 honor crimes have been committed in Turkey between the years 2000 and 2005. According to police records, 29% of these events are due to issues of honor, 29% due to disagreements within the family, 15% due to extra-marital affairs, 10% due to blood feuds, 9% due to sexual harassment, 3% due to rape, 3% due to disagreement in marriage arrangements and 2% due to other reasons. Unfortunately, it is impossible to accurately determine the number honor crimes. Suicides should also be considered within the framework of honor killings. Because in most of the cases the woman in question is forced to kill herself or she may kill herself knowing what awaits her. The whole question of shame and threats within the community ensures that no one is willing to be a witness and the deaths are usually explained and registered as either accidental or as suicide.

There is a consensus over the fact that crimes of honor emanate from cultural and not religious roots and that they can be found worldwide, mainly in patriarchal societies or communities. However it's also an established fact that they mostly take place within Muslim communities. The paradox is that crimes against women committed in the name of family honor are not sanctioned by Islam and many Islamic leaders have condemned this practice on the grounds that it has no religious basis. In the case of Turkey, it can generally be said that crimes of honor are more common in Eastern Anatolia, within communities where tribal/feudal ties and relations continue to exist. In certain parts of Eastern Anatolia, patriarchal norms and hierarchies can still be found in their harshest and most anachronistic forms and women are denied all of their rights. On the other hand, honor crimes also occur in the big cities of Western Turkey as well as in the major cities of Europe where migrant communities reproduce their traditional cultural norms and practices.

Honor crimes should be contextualized within the larger problem of violence against women in general. Many European women suffer from domestic violence, from crimes that are committed within the conjugal home by the women's spouse or companion. According to a report presented to the Parliamentary Assembly of the Council of Europe on September 16, 2004, domestic violence against women is escalating in Europe and the problem extends to all Council of Europe member states. The report states that domestic violence against women "knows no geographical boundaries, has no age limit, is not the preserve of any particular race, and occurs in every kind of family relationship and in every sort of social milieu." According to a report titled "So-called Honor Crimes" presented to the Parliamentary Assembly of the Council of Europe in March 2003, the so-called "honor crimes" occur and affect a whole spectrum of cultures, communities, religions and ethnicities in a wide range of countries around the world including Afghanistan, Bangladesh, Brazil, Egypt, India, Iran, Israel, Jordan, Lebanon, Nigeria, Pakistan, Palestine, Peru, the United States of America, Turkey, the United Kingdom, Italy, Norway, Sweden, Germany. Also from the same report: Some 5,000 women fall victim to "honor killings" around the world every year. As noted earlier it is impossible to accurately determine the number of honor killings. Because of shame and threats within the community, witnesses are not willing to speak up and the deaths are usually explained and registered as accidents or suicide. In many countries women are not even aware that a crime has occurred and they may sometimes think that the punishment is deserved.

It is clear that the problem of honor crimes in particular and violence against women in general cannot be solved by legal measures alone although legal measures are absolutely necessary, especially in countries like Turkey where laws have for long remained insufficient in protecting women's rights. However, much more importantly, what is needed is a change in consciousness and it can only be achieved through education and economic development. Unfortunately, in Turkey, laws have for a long time reinforced unequal treatment of men and women. There were articles that confirmed women's secondary status and their dependency on men. There were also articles that justified and reinforced certain anachronistic norms and values in society. Until recently, laws were either not sufficient or they were not strictly applied.

As a result of the process of EU membership, important steps were taken. Turkey signed international agreements including CEDAW (Convention on the Elimination of All Forms of Discrimination Against Women) for the protection of the rights of women. Also, there were improvements in the legal framework. There were changes and amendments in the Constitution, the criminal code, the civil code and the laws regarding the family.

In 2004, with an amendment made to Article 10 of the Constitution, the state was made responsible for ensuring that men and women are treated equally. Again with an amendment made to Article 90 of the Constitution, it was made clear that whenever there's a disharmony between national laws and obligations resulting from international agreements, international law will be applied.

The most important changes particularly regarding violence against women and honour killings were made in the New Penal Code that took effect in June 2005. Until then, honor killings were considered to be crimes of extreme provocation, and sentences were often minimal. Indeed, the Turkish Penal Code allowed for a reduction in sentence when the killing is carried out in order to purify the honor of the family. Article 463 of the old code reduced imprisonment by 1/8 when a killing was carried out immediately before, during or immediately after a situation of anticipated adultery or fornication.

With the new law honor killings are defined as a form of voluntary homicide and are punished with life-long imprisonment. There is no reduction in the sentence. Also, according to the new penal code, those family members who encourage another member of the family to commit a murder or to commit suicide will be punished. Those who encourage children to commit a crime will be punished more severely.

It is clear that the problem of honor killings in particular and violence against women in general cannot be solved by legal measures alone although legal measures are absolutely necessary, especially in countries like Turkey where laws have for long remained insufficient in protecting women's rights. The state should adopt appropriate legislative, legal and financial measures in order to prevent and punish honor killings and to assist the victims. However, much more importantly, what is needed is a change in consciousness and it can only be achieved through education on the one hand and economic development on the other.

Currently, in Turkey, there are a number of civil institutions that organize educational programs and consciousness raising activities for both men and women. Education of both men and women is a very important long term goal and it requires the cooperation of state, local governments and civil society.

Reference: Summarized from a talk given by Zulfi Livaneli at NYU, NYC USA in April 2006. Zulfi Livanelli was a member of Turkish National Assembly.

Turkey is one of the countries in which honor crimes occur with alarming frequency. These crimes are justified or explained by the perpetrator(s) on the grounds that the crime was committed as a consequence of the need to defend or protect the family honor. How is "honor" defined? We see that male honor is defined through women. Honor lies in a man's capacity to defend the "namus" of the female; here I am using the Turkish word "namus" which has very strong connotations. A man has honor and a woman has "namus." "Namus" is about virginity, modesty and selfless love. It is a concept which is at the center of a complex web of meanings and practices that structure and control women's relationship with their bodies and with society.

Eradicate Violence Against Women in the Church

Graham Hill

In the following viewpoint, posted on the International Day for the Elimination of Violence Against Women, Graham Hill discusses the results of global research regarding violence against women. Part of the research includes a rising number of claims of women who have suffered physical violence by spouses who hold powerful positions within numerous religious institutions. Hill also details ways in which the doctrine of "submitting to your husbands" is used to justify committed violence against women, and how the damaging views of manhood also create a toxic, violence-prone environment. Hill is the Founding Director of The Global Church Project.

As you read, consider the following questions:

1. How long was the study that claimed that 1 in 5 women experienced physical and/or sexual violence by an intimate partner during the survey?
2. Why is there a connection between intimate partner violence and the church?
3. According to this viewpoint, what can be done to stop violence women face that is perpetuated by those protected by clergy?

"Cut the Excuses—Eradicate Violence Against Women in the Church," by Graham Hill, The Global Church Project, November 24, 2017. Reprinted by permission.

Today, Saturday November 25, is the International Day for the Elimination of Violence against Women.

Global research into domestic and sexual violence reveals some shocking and intolerable facts. 1 in 3 women and girls experience violence in their lifetime. In one decade long study across 87 countries, 1 in 5 women said they had experienced physical and/or sexual violence by an intimate partner in the 12 months prior to taking their survey. "In 2012, almost half of all women who were victims of intentional homicide worldwide were killed by an intimate partner or family member, compared to 6 per cent of male victims."

In another study of women between 15 and 49 years of age in 45 countries, "only just over half (52 per cent) of women who are married or in a relationship make their own decisions about consensual sexual relations and use of contraceptives and health services."

In a recent heart wrenching report by Julia Baird and Hayley Gleeson, clergy wives tell their stories about domestic violence. They share their experiences of rape, humiliation, and fear. They tell of being controlled by their pastor husbands, and being ignored and silenced by churches.[1]

The hashtag #ChurchToo has been gaining momentum on social media. Women (and men) are now using that hashtag to share stories of "being groped, raped, coerced and disbelieved by parishioners and pastors in church communities."[2]

> Do not assume that sexual abuse isn't prevalent in christian organizations and churches. A reckoning is coming.
> —Jonathan Merritt

Christian leaders and churches need to cut the excuses and denials, listen to the survivors of domestic abuse, and act to eliminate violence against women. This can only happen when we confront the way power, theology, sexism and patriarchy encourage sexual and other forms of violence against women.

How Do We Confront and Eliminate Violence Against Women in Our Churches?

Here are things we can choose to do, right now:

Listen hard to women and children, and believe them.

Adopt a posture of humility, and an openness to hear how the Spirit is speaking to us in the voices of the victims. How is God calling us to change, and to confront the practices, systems, cultures, theologies, and opinions that have increased the suffering of women and children?

Recognise that we have a serious problem with domestic and sexual violence in churches, Christian homes, and society. Stop acting as though no problem exists, and stop covering up and ignoring abuse.

Stop clutching at simplistic tools and clichés, that ultimately wound and silence victims, and that serve to further entrench violence against women ("forgive others," "submit to your husband," "read more Scripture," "pray for your husband," and so on).

Repent of the ways we (and our institutions and theologies) have excused, validated, or colluded with abusers.

Confront patriarchal, oppressive, and abusive interpersonal systems, theological traditions, and organisational cultures.

Address the deeper issues of power and control that are at the heart of domestic and sexual violence (and that are at the heart of most forms of abuse in church and society). Remorse and forgiveness aren't going to lead to lasting change, unless we seek a thorough change in how power, respect, equality, control, and honour work in relationships and the church. Sexism and patriarchy encourage violence against women. It's time we also examined how the doctrine of male headship is used to support and excuse violence.

Don't let abusers charm you, deceive you, and evade the consequences of their actions.

Refuse to privilege clerical privacy, power, opinions, and dignity, and choose to honour and hear the voices of women, children, the laity, and the vulnerable.

Help victims regain the confidence that they matter, and are valuable and precious—since they matter, their experience and voice and dignity matters, and any offence committed against them matters and will be dealt with.

Stop rewarding narcissistic, egoistical, controlling behaviours and leadership styles in church and society—it leads to similar abuse in the home.

Address and dismantle the unhealthy use and abuse of power in sexual, pastoral, marital, and other relationships.

Acknowledge when ideas like forgiveness and grace and submission are being warped in ways that damage and silence victims, and are letting perpetrators off the hook.

Don't excuse the actions and attitudes of abusers, and don't excuse the environments and views that encourage and support them.

Encourage people to think for themselves, establish appropriate boundaries, practice healthy assertiveness, and say "no."

Stop seeking quick solutions and hasty absolutions—lasting, true, Christ-honouring change never occurs that way.

Confront the lie that sexual availability is a female's (and especially a wife's) responsibility.

Respect a woman's right to bodily and personal integrity and safety.

Practice reconciliation that seeks forgiveness and healing, but also apology, accountability, restitution, truth-telling, and justice.

Welcome public scrutiny and genuine accountability. Stop acting like public scrutiny is persecution; it's not persecution, it's a chance to embrace deeper integrity, transparency, truthfulness, and witness.

Make discussion about abuse—and action to prevent and deal with it—a priority.

See how domestic and sexual violence affects victims—guilt, shame, spiritual trauma, homelessness, poverty, PTSD, isolation, and more—and respond compassionately, generously, and justly.

As my tribe (the Australian Baptist Churches) say, we must seek to be churches and communities that:

- are safe and secure, where the voices and experiences of women, children, elderly and other vulnerable people are valued
- provide practical help for people experiencing family violence
- empower women to speak, serve and lead in response to God's call on their lives
- understand the broader influences in society that lead to violence, and act to bring about change

Rigorously evaluate the fruit of our theologies, practices, and language. And once we take action to change, we should also rigorously evaluate the effectiveness of our programs and responses.

How Do We Confront Sexism and the Patriarchy in Our Churches?

Violence against women grows in an environment of sexism, patriarchy, and unhealthy use of spiritual and religious power. As my friend Michael Frost says, "don't just say sorry, smash the patriarchy!"[3]

So how do we deal with sexism and oppressive patriarchal systems?

We can choose to acknowledge and confront the way power, theology, sexism and patriarchy encourage sexual and other forms of violence against women in Christian families and in the church.

We can own how "submit to your husbands" and the doctrine of male headship is used to justify and excuse violence against women.

We can examine the ways we have harboured sexism in our own lives and families and churches.

We can consider how patriarchal cultures have silenced and oppressed women and girls. We can repent and change and rip these things out by the roots.

We can refuse to ignore or minimize or disregard sexist views and remarks.

We can demand an apology from those who express such opinions. We can demand a commitment to relinquish these views, and never make such remarks again.

We can speak up whenever public figures make derogatory statements about women and girls, or when they seek to silence them. This is a form of violence!

We can question and condemn all sexist attitudes and remarks (no matter who they come from—colleague, classmate, teacher, friend, family member, politician, or whomever).

We can dismantle dualistic and gendered thinking about roles and capabilities.

We can stop celebrating and perpetuating dysfunctional and damaging views of "manhood" and "femininity" (e.g. comments like "boys will be boys," "she's not very feminine," "be a real man," macho stereotypes, and so on).

We can encourage men to speak up and challenge other men on patriarchal and sexist ideas and actions.

We can challenge, confront, and condemn sexism and patriarchal systems in all their forms.

We can create church cultures that respect and value and listen to women and girls, and treat them with the dignity and respect they deserve.

We can stop blaming women, and acting like sexual and domestic violence is a "women's issue." Patriarchy, sexism, and violence against women impacts everyone, at all levels of society— women, men, and children. Men and women must stand together (as part of communities that also stand together) to eliminate violence against women.

We can live blameless lives (both individually and in Christian community), that glorify and witness to Jesus Christ, and that stand in contrast the destructive, demeaning, derogatory, and divisive spirits of this age.

We can cut all excuses, and repent and change and follow the way of Christ.

That is what we can and must do, so that we eradicate violence against women and girls in Christian families, in our churches, and in our society.

Notes

1. http://www.abc.net.au/news/2017-11-23/clergy-wives-speak-out-domestic-violence/9168096
2. http://www.abc.net.au/news/2017-11-24/church-too-christian-victims-of-abuse-join-social-media-twitter/9188666
3. http://mikefrost.net/metoo-dont-just-say-sorry-smash-patriarchy/

In Afghanistan Women Who Oppose Traditional Order Meet with Violence

Clancy Chassay

In the following viewpoint Clancy Chassay describes the rising epidemic of men attacking women with acid for doing simple things like choosing to go to school or for advocating for women's rights. The author notes that, of the 68 women active in the Afghani parliament, only five have been vocal on the case of women's rights, and much of female silence on this matter is due to the heavy Talibani influence in the region. Many Afghan leaders agree with the Taliban regarding women's rights and continue to pass legislation that limits women's freedom. Chassay has covered conflict zones around the world for The Guardian, The Economist, *and other publications.*

As you read, consider the following questions:

1. Why are conditions worsening for women and girls in Afghanistan?
2. What are the perceived crimes committed by women that men feel warrant spraying them with acid?
3. What can men do to expand women's rights in Afghanistan and the Middle East?

"Acid Attacks and Rape: Growing Threat to Women Who Oppose Traditional Order," by Clancy Chassay, Guardian News and Media Limited, November 22, 2008. Reprinted by permission.

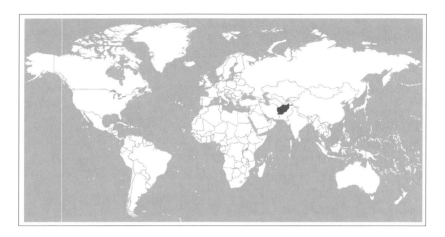

They were walking to school in the southern Afghan city of Kandahar, a group of teenage girls discussing a test they had coming up, when two men on a motorcycle sprayed them with a strange liquid. Within seconds a painful tingling began, and there was an unusual smell as the skin of 16-year-old Atifa Biba began to burn.

Her friend rushed over to help her, struggling to wipe the liquid away, when she too was showered with acid. She covered her face, crying out for help as they sprayed her again, trying to aim the acid into her face. The weapon was a water bottle containing battery acid; the result was at least one girl blinded and two others permanently disfigured. Their only crime was attending school.

It was not an isolated incident. For women and girls across Afghanistan, conditions are worsening—and those women who dare to publicly oppose the traditional order now live in fear for their lives.

The Afghan MP Shukria Barakzai receives regular death threats for speaking out on women's issues. Talking at her home in central Kabul, she closed the living room door as her three young daughters played in the hall. "You can't imagine what it feels like as a mother to leave the house each day and not know if you will come back again," she said, her eyes welling up as she spoke.

"But there is no choice. I would rather die for the dignity of women than die for nothing. Should I stop my work because there is a chance I might be killed? I must go on, and if it happens it happens."

Barakzai receives frequent but cryptic warnings about planned suicide attacks on her car, but no help from the government. Officials advise her to stay at home and not go to work, but offer nothing in the way of security assistance, despite her requests. She said warlords in parliament who received similar threats were immediately provided with armoured vehicles, armed guards and a safe house by the government.

Afghan women are feeling increasingly vulnerable as the security situation worsens and a growing number of western and Afghan officials call for the Taliban to join the government.

"We are very worried that, now the government is talking with the Taliban, our rights will be compromised," said Shinkai Karokhail, an outspoken MP for Kabul. "We must not be the sacrifice by which peace with the Taliban is made."

Under Taliban rule, up until 2001, women were not allowed to work and were forbidden from venturing outside the home without a male escort.

Afghan women who defy traditional gender roles and speak out against the oppression of women are routinely subject to threats, intimidation and assassination. An increasingly powerful Taliban regularly attacks projects, schools and businesses run by women.

Six weeks ago, Lieutenant-Colonel Malalai Kakar was assassinated in her car on her way to work in Kandahar. She was Afghanistan's highest-ranking female police officer and a fierce defender of women's rights. Only five feet tall, she was known to have beaten men she found to be abusing their wives. Another senior female police officer was killed in the province of Herat in June.

Safe house

Talking to the *Guardian* at a safe house on the outskirts of Kabul, Mullah Zubiallah Akhond, a Taliban commander from the southern province of Uruzgan, said the group's attacks on women were

Women's Rights in Afghanistan

Violence against women in Afghanistan reached record levels in 2013, according to the Independent Human Rights Commission of Afghanistan (AIHRC). The six-month period between March and September 2013 witnessed a 25 percent increase in recorded attacks. As Sima Samar, the chair of AIHRC, told Reuters, attacks were more frequent and more brutal, with incidents including "the cutting of [women's] noses, lips and ears," and "public rape."

The struggle to secure women's rights in Afghanistan has been an embattled one. After years of faltering campaigns, the landmark Elimination of Violence against Women Act (EVAW) was passed in 2009 by presidential decree. The unprecedented law criminalises 22 offences, from forced prostitution to denying women their inheritance, prescribes punishments for offenders and outlines a number of state responsibilities. Most significantly, Article 6 enshrines seven victims' rights, including the right of prosecution, legal representation and compensation.

Before the EVAW was passed, cases of violence against women were governed by Afghanistan's penal code, in force since 1976, which contains no reference to violence within the family or underage marriage. Even these scant legal protections were illusory during Taliban rule, when women were denied free movement and access to education and when women were even stoned to death. Since then, Afghanistan has signed numerous international rights treaties and as a signatory is obliged under international law to respond to reports of attacks on women. And yet, according to UN statistics, out of 650 reported cases between October 2012 and September 2013, the law was applied in a mere 109. On average, over the past three years, the EVAW act has only been applied to between 15 and 17 percent of reported cases.

The failure to enforce the law is a chief concern among activists. Speaking to Al Jazeera, Latifa Sultani, an AIHRC spokesperson, recounted a case in which a man evaded justice despite being accused of using an axe to dismember his wife. With perpetrators at large, many victims do not speak out for fear of reprisals, leaving countless women to suffer in silence. Heather Barr of Human Rights Watch accuses the Afghan government of failing women, attributing low rates of law enforcement to a lack of political will.

"Violence Against Women in Afghanistan Peaked in 2013," by Ram Mashru, The Diplomat, January 14, 2014.

always political and not based on any desire to target or punish women specifically.

He condemned the acid attack on the group of schoolgirls in Kandahar, and insisted the Taliban were not involved. "We support the education of girls, but separate from boys. We would not attack schoolgirls. We only target those working with the government."

The Taliban's regional commands have varying attitudes toward women, but all those fighting under the Taliban banner are committed to enforcing their interpretation of sharia law, which forbids women from working or leaving the house without a male escort.

The Islamist group is just one of the many threats facing Afghanistan's few outspoken female MPs. "Our parliament is a collection of lords," said Barakzai. "Warlords, drug lords, crime lords."

In parliament, she says, she is often greeted with screams of "kill her" when she stands up to speak, and she has had no shortage of personal threats from fellow MPs.

They visit her privately to tell her she will be killed if she continues to speak out on such issues as the right of a woman to have a personal passport (separate from the standard "family passport") or against compulsory virginity tests for young women, and the right of a man to have custody of a child at two years old. It is not only men who oppose women in parliament - both Barakzai and Karokhail have faced obstruction from other female MPs on key women's issues.

Karokhail said that, of the 68 women in the 249-strong parliament, only five were vocal on women's issues. The majority of women in parliament vote in favour of more traditional legislation that often rules against women's rights.

Some women now fear the parliament is becoming more conservative towards women. "Talibani ideas are natural among our people, particularly their vision about women," said Barakzai.

According to Afghan commentators, President Hamid Karzai, desperate to win next year's elections, has been bringing former mujahideen commanders into parliament in the hope they will support him at election time.

Most of these former jihadi commanders share the Taliban's ideas about women and are expected to support legislation that will once again limit women's freedom. In addition, according to the Taliban commander, the group has a growing number of MPs in parliament lobbying for their policies.

In much of the country, especially rural areas, women remain subservient to the men in their family and rarely venture out of their homes. Even in the relatively liberal capital, Kabul, it is common to see women robed in blue burkas trailing five paces behind their husbands.

It is difficult to gauge how the worsening situation in the country is affecting women, but according to a recent study by the UN, some 87% of them suffer abuse in the home. Afghan human rights groups are documenting cases of "honour" killings, forced abortions and rape, and a database is now being constructed by the UN.

Najla Zewari, who works for the UN's gender and justice unit, believes violence against women is increasing, fuelled by growing frustrations caused by the economic crisis and lack of security. She said there had also been a sharp increase in rapes by men who claimed they could not afford to pay the dowry needed to marry. After the public shame of an attack, the victim is usually outcast and the rapist is then the only man who will have the woman as his wife.

It is crimes like this that make many Afghans nostalgic for the harsh justice of Taliban rule. Barakzai countered: "Women were safe, in one sense, under the Taliban—but they were kept as slaves, they were not allowed to do what they wanted even in their own home."

As the Taliban strengthen, the future for women in Afghanistan looks bleaker. Barakzai said women's rights, once heralded as the great success of post-invasion Afghanistan, had been sidelined and might suffer more in the struggle to find a solution to the fighting.

Last week, a council of 400 women politicians met in Kabul to discuss this possibility and prepare ways to counter it. Karokhail said: "Our biggest fear at the moment is that the return of Talibani ideas to government will wind back the gains we have made in these last years."

In Nigeria a Terror Group Kidnapped More Than 200 Schoolgirls

Mathieu Guidère

In the following viewpoint Mathieu Guidère details the history of the terror group Boko Haram, and how it transformed into the group that kidnapped hundreds of schoolgirls from the Government Girls Secondary School in Nigeria's town of Chibok. At the time the viewpoint was written, it was not known where these girls were taken, or why they were taken, other than Boko Haram's Islamist beliefs that "Western education is sinful," meaning girls should be punished for pursuing education. Several years later, Boko Haram kidnapped more girls from the down of Dapchi. Those girls were returned one month later, Guidère is Professor of Middle-Eastern and Islamic Studies at the University of Toulouse.

As you read, consider the following questions:

1. What year did Boko Haram reorganize, and what was the outcome of that reorganization?
2. Why do terror organizations choose to target schools that primarily cater to the education of young girls?
3. How are the actions of the group Ansaru similar and different from Boko Haram?

"Boko Haram—The Terror Group that Kidnapped 200 Schoolgirls," by Mathieu Guidère, The Conversation, April 24, 2014. https://theconversation.com/boko-haram-the-terror-group-that-kidnapped-200-schoolgirls-25931. Licensed under CC BY ND 4.0.

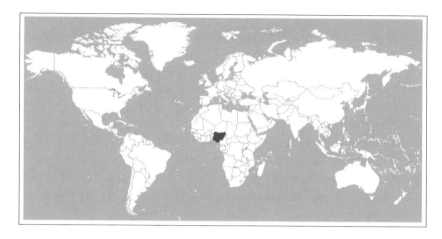

As terrorist attacks go, it was as shocking for its scale and its choice of target: on April 14, at least 200 people were kidnapped from the Government Girls Secondary School in the Nigerian town of Chibok.

More than a week later, the whereabouts of hundreds of young women remain a mystery. Within local communities of Borno province there is much sympathy for parents, but not a huge degree of shock. For this is just the latest in a series of attacks blamed on one outfit: Boko Haram.

To understand the kidnapping, we have to look at the terror group's history, how it was formed, and how its ideology developed.

Boko Haram has made itself notorious with a long campaign of bombings and mass murders across Nigeria, often in concert with other Islamist groups. But to properly understand the group, we have to look at the terrorist group's history, how the group was formed, and how its ideology developed.

In the aftermath of September 11 2001, a 30-year-old man called Muhammad Yusuf founded a new religious preaching group in Maiduguri, capital of Nigeria's Borno State, and gave it the Arabic name "Jamaat ahl as-Sunnah li ad-Dawah wa al-Jihad" (literally, "The Group of the People of Tradition and Call for Jihad"). This group would later become known in Hausa as "Boko Haram," meaning "Western education is sinful."

Yusuf had studied theology in Saudi Arabia and converted to Salafism. He was convinced that the Western education model which prevailed in Nigeria, a legacy of British rule, was to blame for the country's problems; he pledged to fight against it, and to introduce a model inspired by the Taliban's Afghan education system.

The group began as a gathering of Muslim followers at a mosque and at a Koranic school. These gatherings were for poor families to send their children to study a different but parallel curriculum to the existing one: they were taught Islamic sciences, prophetic traditions, Koranic commentary, rejection of Darwinian evolution and the like. The number of these "schools" increased, attracting young adult students who failed in the government universities. They then began calling themselves "the Nigerian Taliban" (Taliban literally means "student of theology").

The core principles of the group were an emphasis on "Hakimiyyah" (sovereignty to God's law); a belief that they are the "Saved Sect," as mentioned in the prophetic tradition of Islam; a contorted interpretation of the edicts of scholars from the classical tradition; and the prohibition of study in Western educational centres or work in any government institution.

The group quickly became politicised and displayed their hostility to the regime of the late president, Umaru Yar'Adua. On December 31 2003, violence broke out in Damaturu, capital of Yobe State, and Boko Haram took control of a number of areas bordering Niger. From 2004 to 2006, violent clashes often erupted between the Boko Haram militants and the security forces, who tried to prevent the group from taking over various schools and public buildings. In 2006, Muhammad Yusuf declared the application of shariah as the main objective of Boko Haram. He was also arrested several times for "illegal gatherings" and "disturbing of public order," though he never faced any harsh consequences in court.

But Boko Haram's real turning point came in 2009.

The Jihadi Turn

In July of that year, a new round of violence began after the group simultaneously attacked four northern states of Nigeria: Bauchi, Borno, Yobe and Kano. The fighting between Boko Haram and government troops lasted for five days in Maiduguri (the Borno State capital), with president Umaru Yar'Adua determined to eradicate the fundamentalist movement. On July 30, security forces successfully expelled Boko Haram from Maiduguri; Yusuf was captured, and then executed in Maiduguri under mysterious circumstances.

Over the next year, the group was reorganised. It forged contacts with major jihadist groups in Africa, particularly with AQIM (Al Qaeda in the Islamic Maghreb) in the north and with the Somali al-Shabaab in the East. Several leaders and commanders left Nigeria and joined the ranks of AQIM or al-Shabaab to train in insurgency tactics and gain experience in terrorism. In July 2010, one of these leaders, Abubakar Shekau, recorded a video message proclaiming himself leader of Boko Haram, and calling for jihad against the politicians, the police, and especially Christians.

Shekhau returned to Nigeria, and in September 2010 launched a spectacular attack, storming a Bauchi prison and freeing hundreds of detained Boko Haram members. Over Christmas 2010, Boko Haram waged a campaign of murderous attacks against Christians. One attack in Jos claimed 80 victims alone.

Despite new president Goodluck Jonathan's willingness to negotiate, Boko Haram continued its armed actions. It claimed responsibility for the suicide bombing against the United Nations office in Abuja on August 26 2011 and the attack at the Christian area of Damaturu that left 130 dead on November 4 2011. Finally, on December 25 2011, the group claimed the attack on a church in Madalla, on the outskirts of Abuja, which killed 27.

Women Used as Suicide Bombers

Islamist terror groups in Nigeria are now using female suicide bombers with babies to avoid detection before carrying out their attacks, officials have warned.

Two women carrying babies blew themselves up in the town of Madagali on 13 January, killing themselves, the infants and four others.

They passed a security checkpoint after being mistaken for civilians because they were carrying children, the BBC reports.

Two other women were stopped at a security checkpoint and detonated their explosives.

Officials told the broadcaster the use of babies could signal a "dangerous" trend.

Islamist group Boko Haram is widely suspected of being behind the attack.

The insurgent group has used scores of women and girls in suicide bombings, prompting suspicions some of those are among the many thousands they have kidnapped over the years.

In one particularly horrific example, a female suicide bomber carrying a baby on her back was shot by soldiers at a checkpoint on 28 November, detonating her explosives and killing the woman and the baby.

On New Year's Eve, a 10-year-old girl was used in a suicide bomb attack in the north-eastern city of Maiduguri.

Boko Haram's seven-year insurgency has killed more than 20,000 people, forced 2.6 million from their homes and created a massive humanitarian crisis.

"Islamist Terror Groups in Nigeria Are Now Using Babies in Suicide Bombing Attacks, Say Officials," by Samuel Osborne, The Independent, January 24, 2017.

Splinters and New Connections

But 2012 was marked by a major split in Boko Haram. In January, the splinter group "Vanguard for the Protection of Muslims in Black Lands," better known as "Ansaru," was formed. The group's motto is "Jihad Fi Sabil Allah": "Struggle in the Path of Allah." In his first statement, Ansaru's leader Abu Usmatu al-Ansari described Boko Haram as "inhuman to the Muslim Ummah [nation]." In another video, the group claimed they would not kill innocent non-Muslims or security officials except in "self defence," and that they would defend the interests of Islam and Muslims not just in Nigeria, but also in the whole of Africa.

Unlike Boko Haram, which is based in Borno State in northeastern Nigeria, Ansaru operates in and around Kano State in northern-central Nigeria, coordinating with the northern Mali-based AQIM and the Movement for Oneness and Jihad in West Africa (MUJAO). It carried out a January 2013 attack on a convoy of Nigerian troops on their way to fight jihadist groups in Northern Mali, and on May 23 2013, it took part in an attack on a French-owned uranium mine in Niger.

Ansaru has also specialised in kidnappings for ransom, with the May 2012 abduction of a Briton and an Italian from Kebbi State, the December 2012 kidnapping of French engineer Francis Collomp in Katsina State and the February 2013 kidnapping of seven foreigners from a construction site in Bauchi State. Leader al-Ansari proclaimed the execution of the May 2012 and February 2013 hostages after a failed rescue attempt by British and Nigerian special forces.

Takfiri Terror

While Ansaru was trying to regionalise and internationalise its fight, Boko Haram continued its terror in Nigeria. On May 14 2013, this led Goodluck Jonathan to proclaim a state of emergency in three northeastern states. Despite this, Boko Haram has not forgotten its priority: attacking "sinful education."

A series of school massacres saw slews of students and teachers killed in the summer of 2013; other massacres were perpetrated throughout the autumn in hopes of starting a civil war. Faced with these massive killings, the army responded with heavy actions against Boko Haram camps.

This caused numerous civilian casualties, and turned local populations against the security forces. By the end of 2013, massacres perpetrated by the army had helped to bring together the splinter groups, leading the more radical leaders of Ansaru to return to the bosom of Boko Haram. The cycle of violence was reinforced.

Since then, the group has moved to the Takfiri ideology, declaring other Muslims as well as Christians as infidels and unbelievers and allowing their murder without any discrimination whatsoever.

Northern Nigeria continues to see an explosion of massacres, a series of attacks that have killed hundreds and show no sign of abating—culminating in the April 14 abduction of hundreds of schoolgirls. Boko Haram's campaign of murder and violence shows no sign of abating.

Periodical and Internet Sources Bibliography

The following articles have been selected to supplement the diverse views presented in this chapter.

AFP, "Boko Haram: Security Fears Keep Kidnapped Schoolgirls at Home," Punch, May 22, 2018. http://punchng.com/boko-haram-security-fears-keep-kidnapped-schoolgirls-at-home/

Feranak Amidi, "Why Iranians Are Sharing Their #MeToo Moments," BBC News, June 2, 2018. https://www.bbc.com/news/world-middle-east-44313751

Julia Baird, "Churches Can No Longer Hide Domestic Violence," New York Times, May 10, 2018. https://www.nytimes.com/2018/05/10/opinion/churches-can-no-longer-hide-domestic-violence.html

Sujoy Dhar, "Acid Attacks Against Women in India on the Rise; Survivors Fight Back" USA Today, July 27, 2017. https://www.usatoday.com/story/news/world/2017/07/27/acid-attacks-women-india-survivors-fight-back/486007001/

Fresno Bee Editorial Board, "Fresno's Domestic Violence Problem Is Overwhelming. But We Must Confront and Solve It," Fresno Bee, May 27, 2018. http://www.fresnobee.com/opinion/editorials/article211958024.html

Tom Gjelten, and Rachel Martin, "Southern Baptist Leader Removed from Post Over Comments on Domestic Abuse," NPR, May 23, 2018. https://www.npr.org/2018/05/23/613636487/southern-baptist-leader-removed-from-post-over-comments-on-domestic-abuse

Arslan Iftikhar, "Honor Killings Are a Global Problem," Time, July 29, 2016. http://time.com/4415554/honor-killing-qandeel-baloch/

Terry Mattingly, "Southern Baptists and Domestic Violence: It's a Tough Issue to Cover After Twitter Explosion," Get Religion, May 1, 2018. https://www.getreligion.org/getreligion/2018/4/30/southern-baptists-and-domestic-violence-its-a-tough-issue-to-cover-after-twitter-explosion

Evelyn Nieves, "Capturing the Strength of Women Who Survived

Acid Attacks in Colombia," *New York Times,* May 24, 2018. https://www.nytimes.com/2018/05/24/lens/capturing-the-strength-of-women-who-survived-acid-attacks-in-colombia.html

Chika Oduah, "'She Refused to Convert to Islam,' 85 Days on, Kidnapped Schoolgirl Leah Sharibu Remains in Captivity," CNN, May 15, 2018. https://www.cnn.com/2018/05/15/africa/boko-haram-lone-school-girl/index.html

Pamela Raghunath, "India's Top Court Orders Scheme to Compensate Victims of Acid Attacks," Gulf News India, June 3, 2018. https://gulfnews.com/news/asia/india/india-s-top-court-orders-scheme-to-compensate-victims-of-acid-attacks-1.2220846

**GLOBAL**VIEWPOINTS

CHAPTER 4

How to Stop Violence Against Women Around the World

In Mexico Public Transportation Is a Threatening Environment for Women

Bianca Bianchi Alves and Karla Dominguez Gonzalez

In the following viewpoint, Bianca Bianchi Alves and Karla Dominguez Gonzalez discuss the implementation of a private project that was implemented in Mexico City, Mexico, to help curb violence against women on public transportation. The authors go on to detail numerous suggestions for future interventions, and also multiple marketing campaign options that are focused on giving rise to a Mexico City where women can go about their lives without being harassed. Alves is a gender specialist with experience mainstreaming gender into transport and social protection projects. Gonzalez has a PhD in Transport Engineering and is an Urban Transport Specialist.

As you read, consider the following questions:

1. What does the proposed intervention entail, and is it enough to curb violence against women on public transportation?
2. What are the intrinsic issues with framing women a man's wife, daughter, or sister, in regard to stopping violence against women?
3. Are there benefits to marketing campaigns that emphasize that women are not "asking for it" no matter how they are dressed or behave?

"'No One Helps…nadie me hace el paro'; Preventing Violence Against Women in Public Transport," by Bianca Bianchi Alves and Karla Dominguez Gonzalez, The World Bank Group, March 8, 2016. Reprinted by permission.

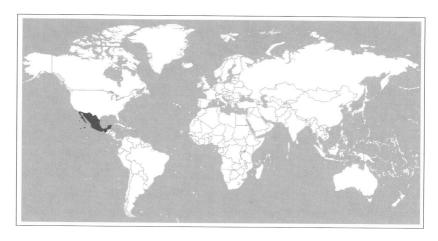

A s a young woman, I feel powerless and exposed when a man
harasses me in the bus. One feels more vulnerable because
people don't react to the situation. No one helps … NADIE ME
HACE EL PARO."

The above-mentioned quote comes from a sixteen-year-old
girl who participated in one of the focus groups organized by the
World Bank for a pilot project to prevent violence against women
and girls (VAWG) in Mexico City's public transport. What she and
other women described about their experience was clear: when we
are harassed no one does anything. The name of this pilot project
reflects that: "Hazme el Paro" which is a colloquial expression in
Mexico to say "have my back."

The focus group discussion, part of an exercise to design a
communication campaign, allowed us to discover that bystanders
refrain from intervening not because of lack of will, but because
they do not know what to do without putting themselves at risk.
That's when the project team saw a unique opportunity to try to
give public transport users tools to enable them to become active
interveners without violent confrontation.

The proposed intervention has three components:

1. A marketing campaign, which provides information to
    bystanders about what they can do to interrupt harassment
    in a non-confrontational way

2. Training for bus drivers on non-confrontational strategies for intervening when harassment occurs, and,

3. A mobile application, which enables bus users to report when they are either victims of harassment or witnesses to it.

Once a passenger reports an event (ranging from verbal to physical abuse) and requests help, a system alert is created and the information is sent to the center of operations of the bus company and a progressive action protocol is followed. Action ranges from broadcasting a warning message through the sound system, to the driver actually stopping the bus and calling the police. Experience shows that just sending a message through the system makes people aware and creates public shame that contains the harassing behavior.

This project was recently launched in Mexico City, and the impact will be rigorously evaluated. So far, the program design has generated relevant lessons for future interventions, including:

- Involve local organizations in the project design and implementation. Working with local gender advocacy and transport NGOs allowed us to adapt our course on Sexual Harassment Appropriate Response Program (SHARP) to Mexico City's social and cultural context.

- Engage the private sector. An ICT company, for example, contributed to the initiative by providing Wi-Fi inside the buses.

- Make campaigns appealing to the local culture. From our discussions with local NGOs and bus users, we agreed to use the phrase "Hazme el Paro" to capture the attention of the community instead of using technical language typically associated to informative campaigns. People were just more engaged when they heard messages with familiar or casual language.

- Baseline surveys helped the design too. From our baseline survey with transport users, we identified that both men and women think that female passengers are harassed because they are "asking for it" (i.e. how they dress, look, or behave). The campaign also challenges that pervasive social norm, with the following message: "women don't like it; women don't ask for it."

- Participatory projects create ownership. Ownership is essential when engaging on projects that touch upon sensitive issues like harassment. After an awareness-raising session, for example, the drivers created their own Action Protocol to intervene in non-confrontational ways to address sexual harassment cases. They saw themselves as key actors of the project, enhancing their commitment.

- Pilot programs are apparently easier to implement with the formalized transport sector. The coordination of the bus drivers or installation of Wi-Fi equipment in the buses would not have been possible without a centralized management. These pilot projects have the added value of generating lessons that will enable a push for broader implementation.

- Take risks and innovate. Different forms of segregated or women only modes of transportation have been designed for cities around the world. While these can be a quick solution, long lasting strategies are much more needed.

Besides these lessons, we also identified important challenges:

1. Be sensitive to organizational concerns. From the focus groups with the bus drivers, it was clear that to trigger a behavioral change in them and turn them into interveners, some of their working conditions also needed to be improved. The challenge was to help them deal with these issues without alienating the bus company, which has been a key partner for the pilot project.

2. Changing norms and attitudes takes time. Behavioral change is not quickly attainable. For countries like Mexico where patriarchy is still very strong, there is need to create interventions to change norms, attitudes and behavior; this is why engaging different stakeholders is essential. Training for drivers and bus company staff should be frequent, but also key for the surrounding community.

3. Scaling up and sustainability. It was easy to engage the bus company to participate in the project. They understood the relevance of it but also their marginal cost was almost zero. Therefore, if we are to scale up the pilot, the bus company should see the real economic benefit of doing so; thus providing the private sector with a business case can be a good entry point.

4. What works vs. what is normatively correct? One of the posters makes reference to a girl that says "Hazme el Paro! I could be your daughter!" This kind of message can be controversial as all girls and women have the right to a life free of violence, regardless of whether they are a "daughter, mother or sister." However, when tested, this message clearly worked for the drivers and the male bus users. It is then advisable to test all the different messages before they are publicly used.

We look forward to the final evaluation results of this pilot and are willing to build on our learning regarding what works and what doesn't to address violence against women and girls in public transport. We are certain that this experience can be valuable to other cities with similar contexts.

Sex Segregation Fails to Address the Root of Sexual Harassment

Holly Kearl

In the following viewpoint, Holly Kearl details the ways in which women-only transportation does not do enough to end harassment. In 2015, U.K. Labor leadership candidate Jeremy Corbyn suggested implementing women-only transportation options as part of his plan to end street harassment, but Kearl points out that that plan excludes LGBTI individuals, not just women, who also face harassment. Kearl details that the point requires a shifting of the male mindset, not the female, to ensure that women have the ability to be in public without facing harassment. Kearl is the founder of the nonprofit Stop Street Harassment and a consultant for the U.N. and Aspen Institute.

As you read, consider the following questions:

1. How many countries have some form of sexually segregated public transportation? Does this do enough to address the root of the issue?
2. Why is street harassment not something women should just "get over"?
3. Per the viewpoint, why does women-only transportation not work?

"Actually, No: Women-Only Transportation Won't End Harassment," by Holly Kearl, TakePart.com, August 31, 2015. This is displayed with the permission of Participant Media, LLC ©2018 Participant Media, LLC. All rights reserved.

L ast week, U.K. Labour leadership candidate Jeremy Corbyn revealed an "end street harassment" plan. Among his suggestions include ones that I support—such as running public awareness campaigns and ensuring that public safety concerns are represented and addressed by local and national political leaders—and one in particular that I do not: women-only public transportation. I'm not alone, and the suggestion has generated heated debate in the U.K. and beyond.

Street harassment has long been considered a compliment or a minor annoyance; something people should just "get over." But many groups and people are now disagreeing with this characterization. Corbyn is the latest high-profile person to say it is a serious issue. While it's wonderful he is acknowledging that street harassment is a problem, he wrote that he would consider women-only public transportation, an idea he said "some women have raised with me." I find this problematic.

Women-only public transportation is a topic I have researched and thought about a lot as the founder of the nonprofit Stop Street Harassment, as a U.N. consultant for the Safe Cities Global Initiative, and as the author of a master's thesis and three books about street harassment.

From unwanted sexual comments on the street to groping on the subway, street harassment is a global problem that limits harassed persons' ability to safely and comfortably navigate through public spaces.

Sex segregation on public transit is not a new idea. Because sexual harassment in public spaces is so prevalent, major cities in more than 15 countries have it. Countries with women-only bus services include Bangladesh, Guatemala, India, Indonesia, Mexico, Pakistan, Thailand, and the United Arab Emirates. Women-only subway cars or sections of trains are found in countries including Brazil, Egypt, Iran, Japan, Malaysia, Mexico, Nepal, and Russia.

When I attended a United Nations forum on safe cities issues in Delhi, India, in June, there were people from several countries who voiced support for women-only public transportation.

A 2014 YouGov poll conducted in 16 major cities, which found that sexual harassment is a problem in them all, also found that nearly 70 percent of women surveyed would feel safer in single-sex areas on buses and trains. Women in Manila were most in favor of single-sex transport (94 percent), followed by Jakarta, Mexico City, and Delhi. In contrast, women in New York saw the least need for it (35 percent supported it), followed by women in Moscow, London, and Paris.

No doubt when you face extreme crowds and constant harassment, anything that offers respite will sound appealing. I thought so too during a 2012 trip to Cairo when I rode alone in both the mixed-gender and women-only subway cars.

But there are notable issues with the concept and the execution of it that cause me to advocate for other solutions.

First, women-only public transportation assumes sex and gender are binary and does not consider LGBTI individuals. It also does not account for men's experiences with sexual harassment and assault—which, while less common, does still happen. This is especially true for men who are or perceived to be gay, bisexual, queer, transgender, and/or effeminate.

Second, the sex-segregation policy does not prevent men from harassing women at subway platforms or bus stops. Pallavi Kamat, a 2013 Stop Street Harassment blog correspondent, wrote about experiencing and witnessing this in Mumbai, India: "Women continue to face harassment as they board the daily train. This could be in the form of the men's compartment adjacent to the women's compartment from which there is cat-calling and verbal harassment. Oftentimes, as a train stops at a particular station, the men on the platform pass lewd comments and whistle at women."

Thus, freedom from harassment in the women-only cars is not even guaranteed. In both Delhi and Cairo, it is not uncommon for women to have to shoo away men trying to ride in their space.

Third, not all women can use these public transport options, as they are often only offered during rush hour, on the major bus lines, and in a few subway cars, leaving many women to fend for themselves in mixed-sex cars. In 2010 in Japan, women vented during a street harassment workshop that sex-segregation "doesn't solve anything." One woman said, "Women who choose to not travel by ladies-only coaches are seen as fair game sometimes. The 'why are they here if not to be felt up' logic."

Fourth, it does not address the root issue of why harassment is happening and thus does not solve the problem. It simply places the onus on women to protect themselves instead of on harassers to stop their behavior. Notably, a decade after Tokyo launched women-only subway cars, the 2014 YouGov poll ranked Tokyo among the top five cities in the world for the most physical harassment on public transportation.

As Julie Babinard, a senior transport specialist from the World Bank, said last year, "Women-only initiatives are not likely to provide long-term solutions as they only segregate by gender and provide a short-term remedy instead of addressing more fundamental issues."

I applaud any person, including politicians like Corbyn, who wants to address street harassment. It is a complicated, pervasive issue that has been seen as normal for a long time. But instead of sex segregation, I suggest what I know is a harder ask: Start with education in schools about all forms of sexual harassment, about respect, consent, and what one's rights are if one faces harassment.

We need public service campaigns encouraging communities to not tolerate harassment and to speak out when friends, family, and colleagues engage in inappropriate behavior. And we also need media outlets and companies to stop portraying street harassment as a joke or compliment in television shows, movies, songs, and advertising.

It will be a long road to completely shift the normalization of sexual harassment, but that road will be even longer if we add a detour to implement the Band-Aid solution of women-only public transportation.

In the United States Respecting Women's Health Will Address the Rising Maternal Mortality Rate

Annalisa Merilli

In the following viewpoint Annalisa Merilli examines one of the least known facets of American society: new mothers in the United States face the highest mortality rates in the developed world. One issue is a lack of documentation of maternal heath, and the fact that women in the United States are not getting the medical attention that they need. Not only do women face many dangers when having children, women of color, especially black women, are much more likely to die in childbirth, at the rate of 79.8 per 100,000 live births. Merilli is a reporter at Quartz.

As you read, consider the following questions:

1. How does a lack of proper medical treatment for both women and new mothers connect to other forms of violence against women?
2. What has led to the decline in maternal health in the United States?
3. What impact does race have on women's health in the United States?

"What's Killing America's New Mothers?" by Annalisa Merilli from Quartz by Atlantic Monthly Group, Inc. Reproduced with permission of Atlantic Monthly Group, Inc. in the format Educational/Instructional Program via Copyright Clearance Center.

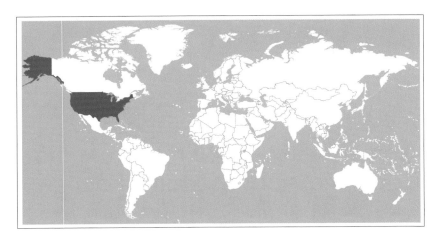

Elizabeth "Liz" Logelin was a young, fit woman with a promising career in operations management at Disney. On March 24, 2008, after a complicated pregnancy that saw her bedridden for nearly two months (three weeks of which were in the hospital), she delivered her daughter Madeline ("Maddy") through an emergency cesarean section. Two and a half months early, Maddy was healthy, if tiny. Twenty seven hours after the delivery, Liz was finally cleared to hold her firstborn. Her husband Matt Logelin already was, he teased her, several diaper changes ahead of her. She got up from the bed, ready to make her way to the nursery, and stopped in front of the mirror. "My hair looks like s---," she said, of her long tresses. She laughed, Matt laughed, the nurses laughed. He thought her hair looked great.

She walked towards the wheelchair that was going to take her to the nursery, and suddenly didn't feel well. "I feel lightheaded," she complained. Moments later, at age 30, Liz was dead.

The cause was a pulmonary embolism—a blood clot that travelled from her leg to her lungs, and killed her instantaneously.

Though she had a family history of blood clots, suggesting a genetic predisposition, and her risk was increased by the prolonged bed rest and the subsequent c-section surgery, to Matt's knowledge Liz wasn't given anticoagulant medications, or advised to exercise to help stimulate her blood flow. Everyone's attention, hers included, was turned elsewhere, to baby Maddy—so precious, so perfect.

There's an assumption that death from childbirth is just not something that happens—not in America, or at the very least not in Matt and Liz's America. "We were very healthy people living in Southern California, with great jobs; [Liz] was very healthy—she didn't smoke, she barely drank," Matt says. "We thought we were untouchable," he adds ruefully.

But dying of childbirth, Matt would learn in the worst possible way, did happen in America. Even to women as young and healthy as Liz, with access to good medical care, and the wherewithal to understand and follow up on their doctor's advice.

On that March day, she joined one of the US's most shameful statistics. With an estimated 26.4 deaths for every 100,000 live births in 2015, America has the highest maternal mortality rate of all industrialized countries—by several times over. In Canada, the rate is 7.3; in Western Europe, the average is 7.2, with many countries including Italy, Norway, Sweden, and Austria showing rates around 4. More women die of childbirth-related causes in the US than they do in Iran (20.8), Lebanon (15.3), Turkey (15.8), Puerto Rico (15.1), China (17.7), and many more.

While most of the world has drastically reduced maternal mortality in the past three decades, the US is one of just a handful of countries where the problem worsened, and significantly.

Between 700 and 1,200 women die from complications related to pregnancy or childbirth every year in the US. Fifty times that number—about 50,000 in all—narrowly escape death, while another 100,000 women a year fall gravely ill during or following a pregnancy.

The dire state of US data collection on maternal health and mortality is also distressing. Until the early 1990s, death certificates did not note if a woman was pregnant or had recently given birth when she died. It took until 2017 for all US states to add that check box to their death certificates. Calculating the number of near-deaths and severe illnesses related to pregnancy is still guesswork. There is no standard or official method of tracking, and cases are not routinely documented. In other words, data collection about maternal health and mortality is a complete mess. Even gathering reliable data for this story was difficult. Quartz was forced to turn to state data where there was a lack of national data, and to supplement gaps of any data with anecdotal evidence. If the US does not know it faces a crisis, how can it reverse the tide, and prevent the needless death of the next Liz Logelin?

Quartz probes the sorry state of US maternal data in a separate story.

The lack of proper documentation of maternal health is about more than data collection though, and speaks volumes about what little thought or consideration has been given to expectant and new mothers in the US. It's hard to avoid the inference that they're not considered important enough to merit focused attention. It's certainly representative of a bigger problem, that women in the US are not getting the medical attention they need. It's as though the US is rendering its mothers invisible.

"It's the biggest catastrophe that we have in medicine to have young mothers die of preventable causes," says Elliot Main, the medical director of the California Maternal Quality Care Collaborative (CMQCC).

Determining exactly why so many American mothers are dying of, or suffering through, pregnancy is a gargantuan public-health puzzle. Through the course of reporting this story, it quickly became apparent that there is no single reason, but instead a complex brew of factors that, together, point to deep-rooted, systemic problems that run through the entire social and health care system of the country. Gender, class, race—and across all, a fragmented, mainly private health system—conspire to work against maternal health. In many ways, it's a litmus test of the health of health care in the US.

Older, Fatter, Sicker: The Fault of the Mothers

America didn't always fare so poorly in maternal health. Like most other developing countries, in the decades following the end of World War II, maternal mortality rates dropped across the US—until the late 1980s, when the trend began to reverse.

Historic data from the Centers for Disease Control and Prevention (CDC) show that right around the turn of the millennium, the US diverged from most countries' focus on policies to curb maternal mortality in a drive to comply with a United Nations commitment to cut deaths by three quarters globally by 2015. Though the global target was missed, maternal mortality fell dramatically around the world—30% according to more conservative estimates, 45% per the official UN report—between 1990 and 2015. In the US, maternal mortality rose nearly 60% over the same period.

Given the inadequacy of the data collected in the US over those years, it's very possible that the country was undercounting its maternal mortality rates all along, and that the increase wasn't an increase at all, but simply reflected better data. Regardless, says David Goodman, senior scientist for the CDC's Maternal and Child Health Epidemiology Program, "At best [maternal mortality] is going flat, but it's still higher than it should be."

Other, related trends were evident in the US over that 1990-2015 period, in particular steep increases in the rates of obesity and diabetes. Couple that with a growing trend of women deciding to delay motherhood until they were older, and you very quickly arrive at a refrain that is often used to explain why America is failing to keep its number of maternal deaths at acceptable levels: that new mothers are "older, fatter, and sicker."

"The increasing number of women who enter pregnancy with higher rates of obesity, hypertension, diabetes, abnormal placentation…are typically the first and only factors considered," points out Christine Morton, a researcher at the CMQCC, in a commentary paper.

In other words, she notes, it's presented as the women's fault.

In a culture that places such emphasis on the value of self-determination and personal responsibility, it's perhaps not surprising that expectant or new mothers would be judged deficient in their apparently poor life choices. But that ignores the fact that increased rates of obesity and related chronic health conditions are global, not just American, and that in other countries, they do not amount to a death sentence. Obesity among white mothers worldwide nearly doubled between 1980 and the early 2010s. Maternal deaths nearly halved.

Suellen Miller, a professor of gynecology and director of the Safe Motherhood Project at the University of California-San Francisco (UCSF), told Quartz that "all over the world, there is an obstetric demographic shift to older women, to more obese women, to women with more chronic conditions, and in many places to women who smoke." And yet, outside of the US, many women are safely delivering babies despite conditions that, some years ago, would have made that impossible. In certain parts of the world—Scandinavia and Western Europe, in particular—a focus on more dedicated care, before, during, and after birth leads to dramatically different results.

It's not enough to say "that women are entering pregnancy 'older, fatter and sicker,' although that may be part of the story," Morton insists. Instead, we need to understand why American women are fatter and sicker in the first place, and why manageable conditions end in women dying.

Priority Matters

Whether they are pregnant or not, women are second-class citizens when it comes to health care. They wait longer to be seen by doctors than male counterparts, their pain is routinely minimized (by gynecologists, no less), and though they are less likely to seek medical attention than men, their symptoms are more frequently dismissed as superficial—for instance being attributed, mistakenly, to psychological rather than physiological causes. Serious health conditions, from heart attack to cancer, are often downplayed in female patients.

When it comes to pregnant women, this manifests itself in a focus on the child, at the cost of a focus on the mother, as highlighted in a recent investigation by NPR and ProPublica into the issue. Health-care professionals spend their time and energy on the baby. This was the experience of the Logelin family—in the end, it was a case of the woman not being fully seen or heard by the US medical system.

Jen Albert, a communications professional from Philadelphia who nearly died after developing polyhydramnios (excess of amniotic fluid) and being induced, says her experience taught her that "no one expects that someone could die in childbirth." The only potential risks that are taken seriously, she says, are the child's, while "the mother is only a vehicle to bring the baby."

Evidence of the US's medical (and social) priorities can be seen everywhere, including in the disproportionate amount of care a woman receives while pregnant compared to after she has delivered. American women typically have three to five ultrasounds of their fetus, for instance, compared to the two or three British (and most other European) women have. After birth, it's a different story. Many other countries (including the UK) provide support from nurses and doulas after a woman has left the hospital, while that's rarer in the US. Meanwhile, the US is the only rich country that doesn't mandate maternity leave.

Women feeling unheard were among the findings of a 2013 maternity care policy report, "Listening to Mothers." Researchers, led by Eugene Declercq, a professor of community health science at Boston University, surveyed 2,400 women who had recently given birth in the US. The results suggested that most women didn't always feel fully supported through their pregnancy. The majority of women reported holding back from asking questions of their providers because they felt rushed (30%)

or they wanted a different kind of care than the one chosen by their doctors (22%), with 23% women saying they held back due to fear of being considered "difficult."

An especially striking example can be found in the way mental health issues—the most common pregnancy-related complication in the US, affecting over 14% of pregnant women—are handled.

In 2016, the US Preventive Services Task Force, an independent panel of experts established in 1984 to decide which preventive measures should be adopted by doctors in the US, recommended that all pregnant and postpartum women be screened for depression. This marked a big step forward given that suicide is the second leading cause of death among postpartum mothers. But a pregnant or postpartum woman who finds herself in need of mental health support still has to navigate a complex process of getting treatment, including waiting lists and screenings, said Joy Burkhard, who leads 2020 Mom, an organization focused on improving maternal mental health care in the US.

Once the baby is born, new mothers in the US generally have to wait six weeks for their first post-delivery obstetrician-gynecologist (OB-GYN) appointment, so even if their doctor is trained to recognize symptoms of depression (which isn't common) those first symptoms of depression that can follow delivery will be missed entirely. This contributes to a vast underdiagnosis of postpartum depression (only 50% cases are recognized in the US) and undertreatment of the condition (15% receive treatment). Suicide accounts for 20% of postpartum deaths.

Too many women report their calls for help being ignored. "I visited 29 care providers, begging for help. I was given so many reasons why I couldn't be helped," remembers Maureen Fura, whose documentary *The Dark Side of the Full Moon* deals with postpartum depression and the difficulties of getting treatment for it. "I was told that my problem was 'too big' for my graduate school's three free sessions of therapy care, that I had to wait three months to be seen, that my insurance was too good, that my insurance wasn't good enough."

It's hard to fathom why, though pregnancy, delivery, and post-delivery are important medical episodes in the arc of a woman's life, her health during those experiences seems to often fall into a blind spot. According to the CDC, as many as 17% of the pregnancy-related deaths caused by blood clots—like Liz Logelin's—could be prevented with simple measures such as compression stockings, or anti-coagulants post-surgery. Such precautions are typically employed after other kinds of surgery, yet often aren't after c-sections. It was only in 2011 that the American College of Obstetricians and Gynecologists (ACOG) postpartum guidelines were updated to recommend anticoagulant therapies following a c-section.

Birthing While Black

Even within a health system that cares poorly for new mothers, the Logelins were somewhat right to think of maternal mortality as something that happened to other people. It typically does.

Black mothers, for example, are three times more likely to die or suffer serious illness from pregnancy-related causes than white women, with at least 40 deaths per 100,000 live births on average, compared to 14 for white mothers. Native-American mothers are nearly twice as likely to die as their white peers.

Black women giving birth in New Jersey, where mortality rates are highest for them, are more likely to die of childbirth—at a rate of 79.8 per 100,000 live births—than women living in some developing regions of the world.

Many other states, such as New York (57), Texas (56.5), Oklahoma (49), produce equally shocking maternal mortality rates among black women. Overall, 33% of white women's pregnancy-related deaths were preventable, according to ACOG. For African-American women, at least 46% of deaths could have been avoided.

Any analysis of race's impact on the rates of maternal death necessarily overlaps with poverty. Black Americans are nearly three times more likely than whites to live below the poverty line, and suffer from the overall health consequences that come with being poor, affecting everything from life expectancy to chronic diseases. But that is just one facet of what's going on. America's Hispanic population, for instance, has rates of poverty comparable to blacks, yet it doesn't experience a similar level of pregnancy-related tragedies. Moreover, major pregnancy complications occur at similar rates for black and white women, yet death and morbidity rates are higher among black women. Education doesn't seem to close the gap, either: Black college graduates experience maternal mortality rates that are three times as high as their white counterparts. In fact they have worse birth outcomes than white high-school dropouts.

"Think about this, we're talking about African-American doctors, lawyers, business executives, and they still have a higher infant mortality rate than...white women who never went to high school in the first place," says Michael Lu, a neonatal specialist. Lu believes that pregnant black women face the stress of a lifetime of exposure to racism, exacerbated by the experience of nine months of pregnancy.

Research backs him up. Institutional racism has been linked to high-blood pressure; black women's bodies pay the consequences of "unique stressors around racism, sexism, violence of any kind, or economic burden," says Fleda Mask Jackson, a professor of public health who led a 2001 study on why African-American women, regardless of their socio-economic background, are more likely to have premature babies. She found that the mother's internalized stress is likely to lead to poor birth outcomes for the baby, and believes it's not unreasonable to infer that those stressors have consequences for the mothers too.

Overall, black women in the US have above-average rates of obesity, type 2 diabetes, hypertension, and experience higher rates of other chronic conditions too. Joia Crear-Perry, an OB-GYN and founder of the National Birth Equity Collaborative, believes that the historical and social causes of maternal mortality, especially among black women, must be taken into account. We have, she says, "a whole language around making it the individual's responsibility without taking any ownership, as a system, of what [society] has done and continues to do."

In other words, the "older, fatter, sicker" refrain will often be applied to black mothers—as a way to hold them individually responsible for problems that date back deep into America's history. Take obesity, for instance, or high blood pressure. Both are often a byproduct of a poor diet, points out Nikia Lawson, an African-American doula and advocate for maternal health based in Fort Worth, Texas. You can trace a line between that poor diet and the historical, social, and economic experience of blacks in the US.

But black mothers die even when they are young, and fit, and educated. Tatia Oden French wasn't poor or unhealthy when she entered the Summit Medical Center in Oakland, California, at the end of December 2001, for a routine check after she had passed the due date for the delivery of her first child, Zorah. Quite the opposite, in fact. A fit, 32-year-old woman with a doctorate in psychology from the University of California-Berkeley, Oden French had an uneventful pregnancy and intended to have a natural birth. But 10 days past her due date, even though neither she nor the baby showed any signs of distress, the personnel at the hospital insisted on inducing labor.

Maddy Oden, her mother, remembers her daughter arguing with the staff that she did not want to be induced, but "finally the nurse said 'well, you don't want to go home with a dead baby, do you?'" This succeeded in gaining her daughter's assent.

"When I asked what [the drug] was," Oden told Quartz, "they said it's perfectly fine, we use it all the time." She said it was only later, after both Tatia and baby Zorah had died during an emergency c-section, that the family was told that the drug, misoprostol, could cause severe side effects, including amniotic fluid embolism, a potentially lethal complication of childbirth that occurs when amniotic fluid enters the bloodstream.

Oden, who is now a doula and an activist against the use of misoprostol to induce labor, believes her daughter's desire for a natural birth was overlooked at least partly because of her race:

"Unless you're rich and white, you usually don't get an explanation of the risks, the alternatives, and the benefits of whatever they are asking you to do," says Oden, who herself is white. (Summit Medical Center declined to comment.)

Oden's deep lack of trust of doctors echoes a sentiment that's common among the US's black population. Elizabeth Dawes Gay, a consultant and writer who chairs the steering committee of the advocacy organization, Black Mamas Matter, explains that African Americans come "from a history filled with abuse and neglect," and it's only "relatively recent generations that interact with the health care [system]."

Their distrust is justified. There is a well-documented race bias affecting the medical profession, and it's made worse by the lack of black medical personnel, in general medicine as well as in the maternity ward: Only 6% of physicians, 4% of OB-GYNs, and less than 4% of midwives are black, versus a general black population of over 12%.

A Matter of Access

While the higher mortality rates of black mothers in the US cuts across class and economic background, a mother's ability to pay for care is nevertheless an important factor in determining the outcome, regardless of her race. A direct correlation can be drawn between not being able to afford care and pregnancy-related deaths and morbidity. Texas, for instance, is the state with the highest number of uninsured people, and the state with the most maternal deaths.

Declercq is currently leading an effort to quantify childbirth practices and outcomes in the US. She says 13% of women who give birth are uninsured, forcing them to pay the cost of childbirth out of their own pockets. Another nearly 50% of deliveries are covered by Medicaid, the federally funded program that pays for prenatal care, delivery, and postnatal care for women who live at 133% or less of the poverty line.

Medicaid for parents, however, typically mandates a lower

income qualification than the program's pregnancy coverage, which leaves many mothers without coverage beyond 60 days post-delivery. But they are still vulnerable well past that timeframe. "Maternal health doesn't just begin [and end] at pregnancy," says Nadia Hussein, an advocate with MomsRising, noting that health care before, in between and after pregnancies is equally important, especially for the 20% of women dependent on Medicaid who suffer from chronic conditions like depression, hypertension, and type 2 diabetes.

While there are no data available covering that 60-day span, the maternal mortality and morbidity task force of Texas found that the majority of maternity-related deaths occurred after the 42nd day post-delivery, and within the first year.

Even for those who can pay the medical bills, there are other ways in which their access to health care is curtailed. For example, of the 3,144 counties that make up the US, more than a third—1,263—don't have an OB-GYN. By 2020, it is estimated the country will be 8,000 to 9,000 OB-GYNs short, largely because the number of OB-GYNs has remained steady since the 1980s, while the population has continued to grow. Financial pressures are, once again, a major reason why. OB-GYNs pay the second-highest malpractice insurance rates after neurosurgeons, reflecting their exposure to a high risk of claims against them. (78% of ACOG fellows have been sued at least once in their career.)

Malpractice insurance premiums can range from $30,000 a year to north of $100,000, depending on whether the state has enforced a cap on claims. This dissuades young doctors from choosing obstetrics as a specialization, and forces many of those who do practice to limit the number of Medicaid patients they see, as the reimbursement rates paid to the doctors are too low to cover the cost of running the business. The OB-GYN scarcity is particularly striking in rural areas: less than half the women living there have access to a hospital offering prenatal services within a 30-minute drive.

Having enough qualified personnel can be a problem in

hospitals, too, which often operate under a financially-dictated "productivity mandate." According to guidelines issued by the Association of Women's Health, Obstetric and Neonatal Nurses, the ratio of nurses to patients in a maternity ward should be one to one for women with complications or women receiving oxytocin in labor, and one to two for uncomplicated women, but it's not uncommon to see nurses attending several patients at once. Even when things go well, new mothers often report struggling to get consistent attention from the nurses, and having only minimal contact with the doctor. "The doctor caught the child, put it on my chest, told me what I needed to do, and went on to deliver the next baby," remembers Tobler of her first birth, which took place in a hospital.

Crear-Perry describes the hospital birthing practice as a mix of "efficiency and fear of litigation." There are, she says, certain delivering techniques, for instance how to turn a baby who's in an inconvenient position for birth, that are no longer taught to OB-GYNs. They are instead trained to turn to surgical intervention whenever the situation isn't straightforward, or if delivery isn't happening within a certain timeframe.

Too Much Is Not Enough

The twin impulses of efficiency and litigation-avoidance result in rushed visits and reduced access on the one hand, and an excess of medical intervention on the other. John Jennings, former president of the ACOG, calls it "the unmet needs of some and the overmet needs of others."

These overmet needs result in what is known in the maternity field as a "cascade of interventions" for many women, even those who would have preferred a natural delivery.

Excessive interventions carry serious additional risks, but they have a deep history in the US. Delivering in the hospital with pain medication became the preferred option of wealthy Americans in the early 1900s, and by the late 1930s the practice of extracting a child from a near-unconscious woman during a "twilight sleep" was

Women's Health Crises

In the developing world, women without access to modern contraception accounted for an estimated 63.2 million unintended pregnancies in 2012. A recent study in *The Lancet* estimated that more than 100,000 women could be saved from maternal deaths each year if they simply had access to effective contraceptive methods. And data from the World Health Organization show that 99 percent of the more than half a million maternal deaths each year happen in developing countries.

Women face health inequities because of their specific needs around sexual and reproductive health care, and because they often lack adequate resources to pay for care. All the factors of gender inequity—including limited access to education, legal systems that fail to protect women, and gender-based violence—are exacerbated by poverty. For these reasons, HIV disproportionately affects women and girls: More than 50 percent of people now living with HIV/AIDS globally are women.

So how does Partners In Health address the particular challenges poor women face? We believe health is a human right for all people—women and men—and that our work must be done in a human rights framework that values participation, empowerment, and equality. This is most evident in our community health worker programs, largely staffed by women, who are tasked with the critical role of educating and accompanying community members. By paying community health workers, PIH engenders economic opportunity and independence that allows women to help feed their families and keep their children in school.

Second, PIH develops programs and health services that address the unique health care needs of women. These include prioritizing broad access to modern family planning methods that meet the specific health and cultural requirements of the population, as well as actively reaching out to women for care before, during, and after pregnancy.

"Women Still Face Big Gaps in Access to Health Care," by Erin George, Partners in Health,
February 1, 2013.

widespread, and remained so until the natural Lamaze movement became more popular in the late 1950s/early 1960s.

"US care is over-medicalized," says UCSF's Miller, and though she acknowledges that it's hard to quantify the impact on the healthcare system, she thinks it's significant. "One of the things [the medical community] is trying to do is swing back to [intervention] 'only when necessary'" she explains, and indeed ACOG's guidelines have been encouraging medical personnel to be more patient, and let labor run its natural course.

That is easier said than done. C-sections, after all, are far more convenient for a hospital. They are easier to schedule, quicker, and make a lot more money; a US hospital can, on average, bill 50% more for a c-section than a vaginal delivery.

Surgical deliveries, however, also come with a higher risk of complications—from blood loss during the procedure to a condition called placenta accreta, in which the placenta attaches itself too deeply into the uterus, potentially leading to severe hemorrhage. Kristen Terlizzi, a healthy, fit woman from California, knows that well. At 33, pregnant with her second child, she gave birth via a c-section. She lost almost her entire body's worth of blood in a postpartum hemorrhage due to placenta accreta, and very nearly died.

According to ACOG records, in the 1970s, placenta accreta occurred in one out of every 4,027 pregnancies; between 1982 and 2002, one in 533 pregnant women developed placenta accreta. Not coincidentally, the incidence of c-sections ballooned over that same period, from 4.5% in 1965 to 32% in 2015. C-sections increase the risk of developing placenta accreta, and each c-section multiplies (table 1) the likelihood of developing placenta accreta in a subsequent pregnancy.

Despite that risk, once a woman has had a c-section in the US, it's unlikely she will have a vaginal birth for her subsequent deliveries. So-called "vaginal birth after cesarean" (VBAC) is safe in up to 80% of cases, yet is chosen by only 10% of women (and doctors) in the US, compared to 40% to 45% in Europe, says Declercq. Typically, the decision to avoid VBAC is based on a desire to lower the risk of uterus rupture—a dangerous condition which requires emergency surgery. But that risk is relatively rare (less than 1% of cases), and c-sections, like all major surgeries, carry their own risks.

Jennie Joseph, a British-trained nurse midwife who has been practicing in the US for the past 26 years and runs Commonsense Childbirth, a birth center which offers midwifery prenatal care in Orlando, Florida, sums it all up effectively: "It's racism, it's classism, it's sexism: All of these things are at play and [...] the intersection with capitalism and power," she told Quartz. "[Women] are dying of a system that's broken."

No Country for New Mothers

If the US was like other rich countries, a health crisis such as this would be met with a flurry of initiatives, spearheaded and mandated at a federal level, to find out why mothers are dying, and to figure out ways to reverse it. But the US isn't like other rich countries. With its uniquely fragmented health system, straddling states and federal government in a complex web of public and private, for-profit and nonprofit, it is nearly impossible to effectively tackle complex issues.

That is not to say the US has no avenues for greater coordination and response. For years, 27 state review groups known as maternal mortality review committees (MMRCs)—some which have sprung from public-health initiatives, others via state OB-GYN societies—have tried to look at available data to assess the causes of maternal death, and if and how they were preventable. "[MMRCs] have existed in the US for a century independently from one another," says Goodman. Five years ago, the CDC embarked on an effort to coordinate this ad-hoc system of state-by-state analysis of maternal mortality, providing guidance to help individual review committees standardize their findings to make them comparable across states. However, the CDC still isn't involved directly in the reviews and, so far, the committees continue to operate independently from one another, says Goodman.

It's a leadership void that in the past few years has been filled in part by a private-sector actor. Pharmaceutical giant Merck has been providing support to a wide range of programs geared towards improving the state of maternal health through its 10-year-initiative Merck for Mothers, launched in 2011.

Though the program was built for developing countries with maternal mortality outcomes far worse than the US, Naveen Rao, the doctor who leads it, says Merck for Mothers was expanded to include the US in response to the poor state of childbirth outcomes in the country.

"The whole idea that in our backyard here is a problem [like this] when we have NGOs that do this work in Africa" was baffling, Rao told Quartz. "Of all the health issues affecting the US, [maternal mortality] is the most unacceptable," he says.

Merck for Mothers has embarked on a flurry of initiatives, partnering with seven organizations in 16 states, and financing projects ranging from better data-collection initiatives to standardized care practices and community efforts to expand health care access.

One project supported by Merck is Review to Action, an initiative to pull together the findings of MMRCs, with the goal of comparing the findings between states. Other efforts focus on deploying simple, standardized post-delivery practices to help identify and prevent some of the avoidable tragedies that afflict high-risk patients.

Main and his team at CMQCC have spearheaded one such effort. They collaborated with a number of hospitals in California to develop three "safety bundles," toolkits that provide a checklist-based set of interventions to address some of the more common complications that occur during delivery. One helps personnel deal with obstetric hemorrhage—from assessing a patient's risk to evaluating the seriousness of the blood loss, along with an inventory of medications, blood units, and tools required for an intervention. Other toolkits developed by CMQCC include ones to address preeclampsia, and a third to promote vaginal delivery over a c-section.

These toolkits have been adopted by over 250 hospital and birthing facilities around the state, and are largely responsible for California's success in cutting maternal mortality rates by 55% between 2006 and 2013.

Despite the clear success of the toolkits, deploying them in hospitals nationwide has been, at best, a patchwork affair. ACOG has worked with over 100 hospitals on safety bundles for hemorrhage, pulmonary embolism, and severe hypertension. A similar project, run by the Association of Women's Health, Obstetric and Neonatal Nurses, is working with 55 hospitals in New Jersey, Georgia, and Washington, DC.

That rollout exemplifies much of what is broken in America's health care system. There are solutions—some of them are even straightforward. But if adopting solutions to discrete, clearly defined problems is this complicated, how is the US going to to deal with the seemingly intractable, deeply-entrenched societal ills of sexism and racism that are embedded in the care its mothers receive?

Current federal and state governments' efforts to improve the health care provided to new and expectant mothers are disjointed and sporadic, and they lack any overarching goal or vision. It's an enormous problem to tackle for sure, but it is also one where the scope for improvement is as great as the gap between maternal mortality rates in the US and other countries of comparable wealth.

Two things are clear: The first is that the US health system needs to render its women, its mothers, fully visible, a process that starts with collecting and publishing more and better data. The second is it needs to see the whole woman, the whole mother— white or black, poor or wealthy, fit or unhealthy—so that the next Liz Logelin and the next Tatia Oden French and all the other new moms get to hold their babies, and to raise them.

In Afghanistan, Palestine, South Africa, Democratic Republic of the Congo, and Bangladesh, Men Are Being Taught to Change Social Norms

Lori Heise

In the following viewpoint Lori Heise argues that violence against women is a global problem, yet we still don't know how to successfully address it. The author discusses an ambitious research program funded by the UK government. In 18 projects around the world, researchers will work with men and boys to address traditional roles. They also will raise awareness of women's rights. The hope is that violence against women and girls will no longer be considered acceptable in these socieities. Heise is Director of the Gender, Violence, and Health Centre at the London School of Hygiene and Tropical Medicine.

As you read, consider the following questions:

1. How many research projects is the UK government funding, according to the author?
2. In what country is the One Man Can project taking place?
3. Why did the focus of combatting violence against women shift from women to men?

"To Stop Violence Against Women, We Need to Get Men to Help Change Social Norms," by Lori Heise, The Conversation, December 10, 2014. https://theconversation.com/to-stop-violence-against-women-we-need-to-get-men-to-help-change-social-norms-35265 Licensed under CC BY-ND 4.0.

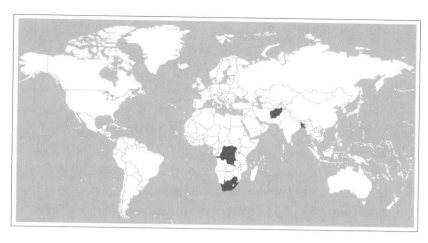

A series of research projects is to take place in countries including Afghanistan, Palestine and South Africa to address our significant lack of knowledge about how to prevent physical and sexual violence against women.

A total of 18 projects will be funded by the UK government, it has been announced. While awareness about violence against women is growing, we still lack good evidence about what actually stops it from happenening and these projects aim to contribute to filling that gap.

The One Man Can project in South Africa, for example, will engage men and boys to challenge traditional models of masculinity. Another in the Democratic Republic of Congo will work with faith leaders to change the social norms that enable violence to continue, and in Afghanistan, boys and girls will work together on peace programmes in schools. Male leaders and families will also be involved in projects that aim to promote an understanding of women's rights, and build healthy relationship skills based on peaceful conflict resolution.

Another project will link international buyers and their supplier factories in Bangladesh with local NGOs to address sexual harassment in garment factories and a national media campaign will be rolled out across the Occupied Palestinian Territories to challenge the acceptability of violence against women.

Wrong Target?

In recent years, attention has turned to engaging men and boys rather than talking to women about how to avoid violence. This approach started with programmes that focused on perpetrators of violence against women. But many women's rights activists were sceptical. Some were concerned that projects like these would divert limited resources away from women's programmes and others warned that they have the potential to further reassert male power, framing men as the protectors and saviours of women.

Now The UN's high-profile He For She campaign is just one example of the projects emerging that call on all men—not just those who are violent – to be part of the solution. They are asked to stand in solidarity with women and make equality one of their own personal missions.

Other projects include lectures and workshops for men to help them redefine what it means to be a man and to have non-violent, egalitarian relationships. Others engage men as bystanders—encouraging them to intervene when they witness other men being aggressive or sexist.

But for all these, the evidence about whether they actually work is limited.

New Ground

It is being increasingly recognised that violence against women and girls is not just about individually violent men. It is a much larger systemic issue. Violence is caused by gender inequality and related to ideas about men needing to be strong and in control.

That means we can't work with men and boys in isolation from the realities of the wider world. To stop violence against women, we need to change the norms and structural gender inequalities in society.

This may include work to change social norms in villages and societies, therapeutic interventions for boys and men who have themselves experienced violence or school programmes about healthy, equal relationships. It might even mean marketing and media campaigns to promote new models of masculinity.

The point is we don't know which stands a chance of having an impact and which wouldn't. These 18 projects can't answer all the questions but they could give us a better idea about what works to bring down rates of violence—and indeed what doesn't.

Through these projects and others we can start to learn more about what works to prevent violence, so that the work to engage men and boys, along with women and girls, can be driven by rigorous evidence. We will all benefit from that.

Periodical and Internet Sources Bibliography

The following articles have been selected to supplement the diverse views presented in this chapter.

Genevieve Bookwalter, "A Year After Opening, Apartments in Evanston for Domestic Abuse Survivors Are 'Making a Difference,'" *Chicago Tribune,* June 1, 2018. http://www.chicagotribune.com/suburbs/evanston/news/ct-evr-ymca-domestic-violence-residences-tl-0607-story.html

Christy Turlington Burns, "Maternal Mortality Is the Shame of US Health Care," CNN, November 18, 2017. https://www.cnn.com/2017/11/15/opinions/op-ed-christy-turlington-burns-every-mother-counts-2017/index.html

Alex Casey, "What Is Being Done About Sexual Harassment on Public Transport?" The Spinoff, May 11, 2018. https://thespinoff.co.nz/society/11-05-2018/what-is-being-done-about-sexual-harassment-on-public-transport/

"Dolonchapa, Women-only Bus Service, Launched," *The Daily Star,* June 3, 2018. https://www.thedailystar.net/city/dolonchapa-women-only-bus-service-launched-1585603

Sheri Gourd, "Victims of Violence Can Turn to New Support Group," *Tahlequah Daily Press*, June 2, 2018. http://www.tahlequahdailypress.com/news/victims-of-violence-can-turn-to-new-support-group/article_186abd60-7bd1-5154-9c85-a6119e8f80f3.html

"In Turkey, a Safe Haven for Syrian Refugee Survivors," United Nations Population Fund, June 1, 2018. https://www.unfpa.org/news/turkey-safe-haven-syrian-refugee-survivors

David Krapf, "Bill Introduced Addressing Sexual Harassment in Passenger Transportation," WorkBoat, May 22, 2018. https://www.workboat.com/news/passenger-vessels/bill-introduced-addressing-sexual-harassment-in-passenger-transportation/

Nina Martin, Renee Montagne, "US Has the Worst Rate of Maternal Deaths in the Developed World," NPR, May 12, 2017.

https://www.npr.org/2017/05/12/528098789/u-s-has-the-worst-rate-of-maternal-deaths-in-the-developed-world

David McGlynn, "In the #MeToo Era, Raising Boys to Be Good Guys," *New York Times,* June 1, 2018. https://www.nytimes.com/2018/06/01/well/family/metoo-sons-sexual-harassment-parenting-boys.html

Leslie Moreno, "Logan County Hosts Weekly Domestic Violence Support Group" Fox Illinois, May 23, 2018. http://foxillinois.com/news/local/domestic-abuse-support-group

Matt Murray, "Congressman DeFazio Introduces Legislation to Combat Sexual Harassment on Public Transportation," NH Labor News, May 18, 2018. http://nhlabornews.com/2018/05/congressman-defazio-introduces-legislation-to-combat-sexual-harassment-on-public-transportation/

Casey Quinlan, "Washington, D.C. Passes Law That Creates Legal Definition for Street Harassment," ThinkProgress, May 31, 2018. https://thinkprogress.org/washington-d-c-passes-law-that-creates-legal-definition-for-street-harassment-c9dfac0f45f0/

Allison Schneider, "Maternal Deaths Are Rising in America. Best Mother's Day Gift, Reverse That Trend." *USA Today,* May 10, 2018. https://www.usatoday.com/story/opinion/2018/05/10/maternal-deaths-mothers-mortality-column/595818002/

Md Sanaul Islam Tipu and Ashif Islam Shaon, "Sexual Harassment on Buses: 'Everyone Must Stand with the Victims," *Dhaka Tribune,* May 19, 2018. https://www.dhakatribune.com/bangladesh/2018/05/19/sexual-harassment-on-buses-everyone-must-stand-with-the-victims

For Further Discussion

Chapter 1
1. How can feminism become a movement that goes beyond political affiliation?
2. Can changing the legal age a woman can get married be a factor in stopping marriage-related violence?
3. How did China's One-Child Rule impact the "missing women" epidemic?

Chapter 2
1. How is "femicide" used differently within the viewpoints in this resource? Is this use consistent, or should other terms be used?
2. Why is femicide such an epidemic in Latin America?
3. Why are women physiologically at a greater risk of contracting HIV?

Chapter 3
1. How does toxic masculinity contribute to religious-based violence in the church?
2. Around the world why is there so much connection between religion and violence committed by men against women?
3. Why is there such a close connection between violence against women and the jihadist interpretation of Islam?

Chapter 4
1. How does gender-segregated transport also fail men who suffer from sexual violence? Who else might not be helped?
2. How much of a difference can something like a badge make to stop the epidemic of men groping young girls in Japan?
3. Why is public transportation such a common place in which women are harassed?

Organizations to Contact

The editors have compiled the following list of organizations concerned with the issues debated in this book. The descriptions are derived from materials provided by the organizations. All have publications or information available for interested readers. The list was compiled on the date of publication of the present volume; the information provided here may change. Be aware that many organizations take several weeks or longer to respond to inquiries, so allow as much time as possible.

Association for Women's Rights in Development (AWID)
215 Spadina Ave, Suite 150, Toronto, Ontario, M5T 2C7 Canada
(416) 594-3773
email: info@awid.org
aebsite: www.awid.org

AWID aims to be a driving force within the global community of feminist and women's rights activists, organizations and movements, strengthening our collective voice, influencing and transforming structures of power and decision-making and advancing human rights, gender justice and environmental sustainability worldwide. Working together is key for women's rights and gender justice to be a lived reality and we support feminist and women's rights organizations and movements to collaborate effectively across issues, regions and constituencies.

Global Fund for Women
800 Market St, 7th Floor, San Francisco, CA 94102
(415) 248-4800
email: info@gblobalfundforwomen.org
website: www.globalfundforwomen.org

Global Fund for Women exists to support the tireless and courageous efforts of women's groups who work every day to win rights for women and girls. These groups are working to ensure women can own property, vote, run for office, get paid fair wages, and live free from violence—including domestic violence, sexual assault, and harmful practices such as female genital mutilation.

Guatemala Human Rights Commission
3321 12ᵗʰ St NE, Washington DC 20017
(202) 529-6599
email: ghrc-usa@ghrc-usa.org
website: www.ghrc-usa.org

The Guatemala Human Rights Commission/USA (GHRC) is a non-profit, grassroots, solidarity organization dedicated to promoting human rights in Guatemala and supporting communities and activists who face threats and violence. GHRC documents and denounces abuses, educates the international community, and advocates for policies that foster peace and justice.

Institut Barcelona d'Estudis Internacionals
Carrer de Ramon Trias Fargas, 25, 08005, Barcelona, Spain
+34 935 24 30 30
email: comunicacio@ibei.org
website: ibei.org

IBEI is an inter-university institute created in 2004 as a joint effort of all five public universities in the Barcelona metropolitan area and CIDOB (International Documentation Centre of Barcelona) to promote postgraduate training and research in politics and international relations in order to advance the understanding of global challenges to governance in our world. Now into its second decade, IBEI has become consolidated and achieved a high level of recognition as an academic and research centre at both European and international levels.

International Alliance of Women
16 Skoufa St, Athlens, Greece
email: iawpresident@womenalliance.org.
website: womenalliance.org

Founded in 1904 and based in Geneva, the International Alliance of Women (IAW) is an international NGO comprising 41 member organizations involved in the promotion of the human rights of women and girls globally. The IAW has general consultative status with the UN Economic and Social Council and is accredited to many specialized UN agencies, has participatory status with the Council of Europe and is represented at the Arab League, the African Union and other international organizations.

International Women's Health Coalition
333 Seventh Ave, 6th Floor, New York, NY 10001
(212) 979-8500
email: info@iwhc.org
website: www.iwhc.org

IWHC advances the sexual and reproductive health and rights of women and young people, particularly adolescent girls, in Africa, Asia, Eastern Europe, Latin America, and the Middle East. IWHC furthers this agenda by supporting and strengthening leaders and organizations working at the community, national, regional, and global levels, and by advocating for international and US policies, programs, and funding.

National Organizationfor Women
1100 H Street NW, Suite 300, Washington DC 20005
(202) 628-8669
email: info@now.org
website: www.now.org

NOW is dedicated to its multi-issue and multi-strategy approach to women's rights and is the largest organization of feminist grassroots activists in the United States.

Pan American Health Organization

252 23rd St NW, Washington DC 20037
(202) 974-3000
email: info@paho.org
website: www.paho.org

PAHO is committed to ensuring that all people have access to the health care they need, when they need it, with quality and without fear of falling into poverty. Through its work, PAHO promotes and supports the right of everyone to good health. PAHO promotes the inclusion of health in all public policies and the engagement of all sectors in efforts to ensure that people live longer, healthier lives, with good health as their most valuable resource.

United Nations Entity for Gender Equality and the Empowerment of Women

220 E 42nd St, New York, NY 10017
(646) 781-4400
website: www.unwomen.org

UN Women is the global champion for gender equality, working to develop and uphold standards and create an environment in which every woman and girl can exercise her human rights and live up to her full potential. We are trusted partners for advocates and decision-makers from all walks of life, and a leader in the effort to achieve gender equality.

Women for Women International

2000 M St NW, Suite 200, Washington DC 20036
(202) 737-7705
email: general@womenforwomen.org
website: www.womenforwomen.org

Women for Women International delivers our programs through the generous support of individual, corporate and foundation donors, partners, and governments. Women for Women International was honored with the prestigious Conrad N. Hilton Humanitarian

Prize in 2006, and receives favorable ratings from independent charity groups.

World Economic Forum
91-93 Route de la Capite, CH-1223 Cologny/
Geneva Switzerland
+41 22 869 1212
email: contact@weforum.org
website: www.weforum.org

The World Economic Forum engages the foremost political, business and other leaders of society to shape global, regional and industry agendas. The Forum strives in all its efforts to demonstrate entrepreneurship in the global public interest while upholding the highest standards of governance.

Bibliography of Books

Lisa Carlson. *End Domestic Violence: The Complete Guide to Red Flags, Abuse, and Healing.* Seattle, WA: Amazon Digital Services, 2018.

Shami Chakrabarti. *Of Women.* London, UK: Penguin UK, 2018.

Rosa-Linda Fregoso, Cynthia Bejarano. *Terrorizing Women: Feminicide in the Americas.* Durham, NC: Duke University Press, 2010.

Judith L. Herman. *Trauma and Recovery: The Aftermath of Violence—From Domestic Abuse to Political Terror.* New York, NY: Basic Books, 2015.

Andy Johnson. *Religion and Men's Violence against Women.* Cham, Switzerland: Springer International Publishing, 2015.

Marti Long, Melissa Scardaville. *Intimate Coercion: Recognition and Recovery.* Lanham, MD: Rowman & Littlefield, 2015.

Matthew Lysiak. *Newton: An American Tragedy.* New York, NY: Gallery Books, 2014.

Hilary Matfess. *Women and the War on Boko Haram: Wives, Weapons, Witnesses.* Chicago, IL: Zed Books, 2017.

Michael A. Messner, Max A. Greenberg, Tal Peretz. *Some Men: Feminist Allies and the Movement to End Violence against Women.* Oxford, UK: Oxford University Press, 2015.

Chris Newman, Kate Iwi. *Engaging with Perpetrators of Domestic Violence: Practical Techniques for Early Intervention.* London, UK: Jessica Kingsley Publishers, 2015.

Traci D. O'Neal. *The Exceptional Negro: Racism, White Privilege and the Lie of Respectability Politics.* Nottingham, UK: iCart Media, 2018.

Steven Pinker. *Enlightenment Now: The Case for Reason, Science, Humanism, and Progress.* New York, NY: Viking, 2018.

David L Richards, Jillienne Haglund. *Violence qgainst Women and the Law.* Abingdon, UK: Routledge, 2015.

Mike Smith. *Boko Haram: Inside Nigeria's Unholy War.* London, UK: I. B. Tauris Publishers, 2016.

Alexander Thurston. *Boko Haram: The History of an African Jihadist Movement.* Princeton, NJ: Princeton University Press, 2017.

Jesmyn Ward. *The Fire This Time: A New Generation Speaks about Race.* London, UK: Bloomsbury Publishing, 2018.

Malala Yousafzai. *I Am Malala: The Girl Who Stood Up for Education and Was Shot by the Taliban.* Boston, MA: Little, Brown and Company, 2013.

Index